WORLD BANK STAFF OCCASIONAL PAPERS □ NUMBER TWENTY-NINE

Farm Budgets

From Farm Income Analysis
to Agricultural Project Analysis

Maxwell L. Brown

Farm Budgets

From Farm Income Analysis to Agricultural Project Analysis

PUBLISHED FOR THE WORLD BANK
The Johns Hopkins University Press
Baltimore and London

Library of Congress Cataloging in Publication Data

Brown, Maxwell L   1931–
    Farm budgets.
    (World Bank staff occasional papers ; no. 29)
    Bibliography: p. 133
    1. Agriculture—Economic aspects. 2. Farm income.
I. International Bank for Reconstruction and Development. II.
Title. III. Series.,
HD1415.B74   636'.01'0681   79–3704
ISBN 0–8018–2386–2
ISBN 0–8018–2387–0 pbk.

Introduction

•-•

I would like to explain why the World Bank does research work and why this research is published. We feel an obligation to look beyond the projects that we help finance toward the whole resource allocation of an economy and the effectiveness of the use of those resources. Our major concern, in dealing with member countries, is that all scarce resources—including capital, skilled labor, enterprise, and know-how—should be used to their best advantage. We want to see policies that encourage appropriate increases in the supply of savings, whether domestic or international. Finally, we are required by our Articles, as well as by inclination, to use objective economic criteria in all our judgments.

These are our preoccupations, and these, one way or another, are the subjects of most of our research work. Clearly, they are also the proper concern of anyone who is interested in promoting development, and so we seek to make our research papers widely available. In doing so, we have to take the risk of being misunderstood. Although these studies are published by the Bank, the views expressed and the methods explored should not necessarily be considered to represent the Bank's views or policies. Rather, they are offered as a modest contribution to the great discussion on how to advance the economic development of the underdeveloped world.

ROBERT S. MCNAMARA
President
The World Bank

Contents

Tables and Figures

•–•–•

Figures

Foreword

In recent years the Economic Development Institute of the World Bank (EDI) has been collaborating with institutions in the Third World to develop a number of training programs for specialists, administrators, and planners in different economic sectors. An important part of the Institute's effort has been to develop appropriate teaching materials and to make them more widely available.

Maxwell Brown, formerly a Chief Agricultural Economist with the Agricultural Planning Unit of the Ministry of Agriculture in Jamaica, has been a member of the EDI staff for six years. This book has grown out of his contributions to the teaching and direction of our courses in Agriculture and Rural Development. It will be especially useful for those in developing countries charged with preparing agricultural and rural development projects, whether financed wholly from national resources or with partial funding from international sources. A most crucial consideration in these projects is whether the proposed production components are remunerative and attractive for farmers and their families. The standard tool for judging the effect on incomes of these projects is the farm budget. This book will also help project designers test whether proposed projects will contribute to overall economic development.

AJIT MOZOOMDAR
*Director, Economic
Development Institute
The World Bank*

Preface

•-•--•-•

There is a wealth of literature on farm income analysis and agricultural project analysis, but little has been published which clarifies the difference between them or which shows how the transition is made from one to the other. The purpose of this study is to bridge this gap, providing theoretical instruction in layman's language and giving practical guidance to those responsible for planning or making investment decisions in agriculture or in the wider field of rural development.

This study is written primarily for participants in courses on agricultural and rural development projects given by the Economic Development Institute (EDI) of the World Bank or by similar organizations. It should also prove useful to students from developing countries, particularly practitioners in the field of agriculture and rural development.

The style and presentation of the subject matter reflect the study's origin in EDI's courses in Washington and in developing countries around the world. The material is presented in a simple and a straightforward way, so that it will be understood easily by a broad cross section of readers—specialists and non-specialists alike. The study is not intended to be a treatise on agriculture, because many of the people involved in planning agricultural projects are not agricultural specialists. Nor does it attempt to be a treatise on economic theory, because most of the specialists who must provide the technical data for agricultural planning have no formal training in economics. Thus, much of the theoretical discussion often associated with farm income analysis and agricultural project analysis has been simplified. The emphasis throughout is on the application of the more practical aspects of project preparation.

Many of the ideas in this study have been inspired by two main sources. The sections dealing with farm income analysis and partial budgeting are built around the techniques presented by the authors of *The Farm as a Business*, published for the Ministry of Agriculture, Fisheries, and Food by Her Majesty's Stationery Office in England. The sections dealing with agricultural project analysis are influenced by close association with J.

Price Gittinger, to whom I am greatly indebted for his encouragement and intellectual leadership as my Division Chief in the Economic Development Institute.

The preparation of this study has benefited considerably from discussions and debates with my colleagues in the Economic Development Institute, particularly William A. Ward, William I. Jones, Orlando Espadas, Arnold von Ruemker, Jack Upper, and J. D. von Pischke. Hundreds of EDI participants in agricultural and rural development project courses held in Washington and other countries have read earlier drafts and offered valuable criticisms. Special thanks are due to Raymond Frost, former director of the Institute, and Bernard Chadenet, vice-president of the World Bank, for their encouragement. I am also indebted to Professor Pan A. Yotopoulos of the Food Research Institute, Stanford University, as well as to the members of the World Bank's editorial committee and its panel of reviewers for their most helpful comments and constructive criticisms.

Josephine Woo did a superb job in transforming earlier drafts from the jargon of the classroom to a style more suited to a wider readership. Tahany Habib had the most arduous task of all, typing and retyping what seemed to be a never-ending stream of drafts. Virginia deHaven Orr edited the final manuscript and managed production of the book, and Pensi Kimpitak prepared the figures.

MAXWELL L. BROWN

Farm Budgets

From Farm Income Analysis to Agricultural Project Analysis

1

•-•-•-•--•

Introduction and Summary

A budget is simply a plan to coordinate the inflows and outflows of resources to achieve a given set of objectives. Farm budgeting is concerned with organizing resources on a farm to maximize profits or, more often, family satisfaction. It is traditionally treated as a branch of farm management economics: a hybrid of accounting, agriculture, and economics. Drawing on the physical, biological, and social sciences, it considers farm organization in terms of efficiency and continuous profit. Agricultural project analysis runs parallel to farm management analysis, overlapping with it in many ways, but also incorporating some basic modifications.

Budgets for farm management analysis are prepared primarily to evaluate the efficiency of a particular farm or a group of farms within a prescribed accounting period, usually one year. In agricultural project analysis, however, budgets provide the basis for evaluating and comparing the relative profitability of alternative investments, which may involve a single farm or a group of farms (described as the project area), in which some clearly defined input or package of inputs is invested, and from which a flow of benefits and costs is projected over a specific period (described as the life of the project), usually lasting several years.

Essentially, farm management analysis takes a microscopic view of each year of the project, whereas agricultural project analysis takes a telescopic view of the entire life of the project. Farm management analysis reflects the efficiency and profitability of the project on a year-by-year basis; agricultural project analysis uses the annual differences between benefits and costs to calculate an index for the profitability of the project over its entire life. This index may be in terms of an internal rate of return, a net present worth, or a benefit/cost ratio.

Figure 1–1. *Stages in Farm Income Analysis and Agricultural Project Analysis*

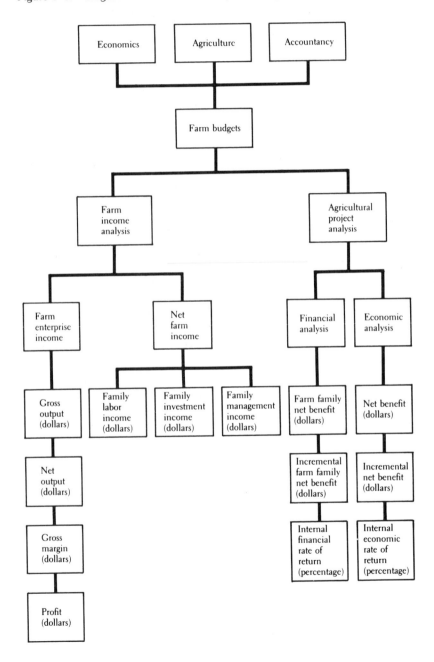

4

This study does not discuss the entire field of farm management. Rather, it focuses on just one aspect—farm income analysis—which is a necessary complement to agricultural project analysis, because it is important to consider the profitability of a project not only in aggregate over the life of the investment but also on a year-by-year basis.

Farm Income Analysis and Agricultural Project Analysis

Farm income analysis reflects the profitability of a farm on an annual basis. It can be approached from two angles: from the viewpoint of the farm as a whole or from the viewpoint of each constituent enterprise. The first approach leads to the calculation of the net farm income, which represents the reward to the farm family for their labor, capital, and management invested in the farm during the particular year being analyzed.[1] The profitability of each constituent enterprise can be measured at various stages: namely, gross output, net output, gross margin and profit, each of which successively takes into account more elements of cost.

In agricultural project analysis, profitability is expressed as an index which characterizes the performance of the project over its whole life, not just one year at a time. There are also two basic approaches to agricultural project analysis: the financial and the economic. The financial analysis evaluates the project in terms of its attractiveness to the farm family or to other entities participating in the project. In the economic analysis the project is considered from the point of view of society as a whole. Figure 1–1 illustrates the distinction between farm income analysis and agricultural project analysis, and shows some of the intermediate stages in each.

Summary of the Study

This study shows the logical progression from farm income analysis to agricultural project analysis, highlighting at each stage the kinds of budgets that are required and the differences in the methodology used in each type of analysis.

Farm income analysis

Chapter 2 begins with an analysis of the structure of the farm industry. Three groups of farms are identified: commercial, subsistence, and semi-

---

1. United Kingdom, Ministry of Agriculture, Fisheries, and Food, *The Farm as a Business* (London: Her Majesty's Stationery Office, 1958), p. 18.

subsistence. The methodologies presented in this study are developed for application to semisubsistence farms, but they can also be used for analyzing commercial farms. The study shows that, even in the absence of the system of accounts available on commercial farms, it is possible to prepare budgets as a basis for calculating the gross output, net output, gross margin, and profit for each enterprise. By aggregating the costs and benefits from the individual enterprise budgets and by making certain adjustments, the net farm income is calculated.

Partial budgets

The farmer uses enterprise analysis to prepare budgets that provide the basis for making management decisions on the farm, such as whether to introduce, expand, reduce, or eliminate certain enterprises and how to adjust the organization of the farm to enhance profitability. Chapter 3 introduces the technique of partial budgeting, which is appropriate only when the contemplated change is so small that it will have a minimal effect on the organization of the rest of the farm.

Transition to complete budgeting and project analysis

When the proposed change is a major one or when an investment will have a long-term effect on the organization, complete budgeting must be undertaken. Chapter 4 shows that the methodology of project analysis overlaps with complete budgeting, although the latter is usually associated with analysis of a single farm and project analysis with a large number of farms. In moving from farm income analysis to agricultural project analysis, the time frame shifts from a particular year to the entire life of the project, and the times when costs occur and benefits accrue assume special significance in the analysis. The technique of discounting is introduced to express costs and benefits over the life of the project in present values, providing a basis for comparison. This chapter also illustrates the calculation of the benefit/cost ratio, net present worth, and the internal rate of return.

Budgets for land, labor, and capital

Chapter 5 discusses the importance of preparing budgets for land, labor, and capital. The land budget helps the farmers to select the cropping sequences and combinations that will yield the best income and enhance the productivity of the soil. The labor budget is particularly important, since labor is usually the most substantial input contributed by the farm family on semisubsistence farms. Labor profiles are first prepared for each enterprise. Then these are aggregated to prepare the labor budget, which shows the supply and demand for labor for the whole farm. A distinction is made between family labor and hired labor, because they are treated differently in the financial, as well as in the economic, analysis.

Capital is discussed as a physical resource (such as equipment, raw materials, and inputs produced on the farm) and as a financial resource representing the monetary value of the items of costs and benefits. A distinction is made between the budget which is required to calculate the rate of return and that which is required to test the liquidity of the farm. When the financial resources of the farm as a business and as a place of domicile are so interwoven that both aspects cannot be differentiated, a budget should be made for the financial resources of the farm-home complex and not merely for the farm.

Farm models

A farm model is a simplified representation of a typical farm included in the project. It is used to typify the different farming situations that may be found in a project. Preparation of farm models serves two important functions: to facilitate analysis of the attractiveness of the projects to different groups of farmers and to prepare for the aggregation of the project's total costs and benefits. The nature of the project will determine the number of models that are necessary. Different systems are used to make projections for crop and livestock models.

Farm models should reflect what each group of farmers is likely to do and not what the analyst would like the farmer to do. Thus, realistic assumptions should be made about the rates of adaptation both in terms of the phasing of the area to be brought under the influence of the project each year during the implementation period as well as in the projection of increases in productivity.

Financial analysis

In this phase of the analysis the models represented in the project are assessed from the viewpoint of those contributing capital to, and sharing in the rewards of, the project. To show the return on the farm family's investment, the rate of return is calculated after financing; so inflows of loans and outflows for debt service are included. In order to calculate the rate of return on all capital invested in the project, the rate of return is calculated before financing, and loans and debt service are omitted from the analysis. The main items involved in preparing the financial analysis are inflows (gross value of production, loan receipts, grants, subsidies, and rental value of the farmhouse); outflows (investment costs, operating expenses, and debt service); the farm family net benefit with and without the project; and the incremental farm family net benefit.

Economic analysis

The economic analysis of a project reflects the profitability of the project from the viewpoint of society as a whole: that is, whether the project makes the most efficient use of the nation's resources in producing national income. It is concerned with the flow of real resources, therefore, transfer payments are excluded. Also, in the analysis, resources are valued in terms of their opportunity cost, which may be different from the price in the market. Therefore, in making the transition from the financial analysis to the economic analysis, adjustments are made to remove distortions in the prices of foreign exchange, inputs, and outputs.

The economic analysis incorporates the off-farm investment costs and provision of common services, which are not included in the financial analysis, and it is prepared either by aggregating data from the farm models and then adding off-farm costs or by aggregating enterprise budgets. In either case, attention must be paid to the phasing involved in implementing the project.

This study is concerned mostly with the calculation of the economic rate of return, because it is the one measure of project worth most commonly used by international credit institutions. The economic rate of return has certain limitations, however, and in circumstances such as comparing mutually exclusive projects, the net present worth is the more reliable basis for ranking projects.

Despite the importance of the economic analysis, economic efficiency is not the sole criterion for selecting projects to implement. Stronger influences are sometimes exerted by social and political factors. But this does not invalidate the importance of the economic analysis, since its value does not lie merely in calculating the economic rate of return, the net present worth, or the benefit/cost ratio. Given the assumptions about government policies and resource availabilities, the economic analysis provides the framework within which the contribution of a project to national income can be evaluated and compared with other projects. But it is the whole process of preparing the budgets and laying out each step of the analysis in a coordinated and systematic manner, so that each assumption can be tested and so that the design of the project can be challenged and improved, that makes the effort worthwhile.

2

•–•

Farm Income Analysis

It is sometimes argued that farming is a way of life adopted only because of family tradition, a desire to be self-employed, a love of nature, or some other subjective consideration. These considerations, however, do not necessarily mean that farmers are neither responsive to price nor motivated by profit. To understand farmers' attitudes, it is necessary to analyze the structure of the farm industry.

The Structure of Farming

Generally, farms can be divided into three groups. At one extreme are corporations, partnerships, and cooperatives with paid management and other characteristics of the commercial firm in the industrial sector. At the other extreme is the pure type of subsistence farm in which the family has little contact with the market. In between is the partly commercial and partly subsistence family farm. Most farms in developing countries belong to this last category. Understanding the principles governing the decisionmaking process on these farms is, therefore, important for the success of any agricultural project designed to contribute to a country's economic development.

The purely commercial farm may be regarded as being motivated primarily by the objective of profitmaking; and the semisubsistence, semicommercial farm, by many objectives that contribute to maximizing family satisfaction. "Satisfaction is increased by the benefits of farm output and decreased by the cost of sacrificing food, leisure, money or taking risks."[1]

1. Martin Upton, *Farm Management in Africa* (London: Oxford University Press, 1973), p. 7.

9

Realizing a profit on the sale portion of the crop is important, but maximizing profit is not always the over-riding consideration in allocating resources. Increased profits increase family satisfaction only to a certain degree. At some levels, profit maximization might be secondary to family satisfaction, and enterprises and productive processes that allow the family greater security and satisfaction might take precedence over those that are more profitable.

The semisubsistence farm can be viewed best as a household-farm complex. A similar relation exists in some small-scale industries, but it is not typical of usual commercial operations in which the family contributing capital to the business is often remote physically as well as managerially from the firm. In contrast, the semisubsistence farm family is a complete economic and social entity. Not only do the members of the family share in the work on the farm, but the well-being of each member directly influences the management of the farm relative to resource allocation, income distribution, and capital accumulation. The strong farm-household relation affects major areas of decisionmaking, such as the choices between income-generating enterprises and non–income-generating activities or leisure; between future and present income; between production for the market and production for the home; between production for a specialized market and production for several marketing possibilities; between family consumption (including education, entertainment, and health) and investment in the farm; and between short-term and long-term enterprises.

This strong farm-household relation may not indicate that farmers lack economic motivation. In fact research results often show that farmers in developing countries are responsive to prices.[2] Similarly, the farmer's choice to produce traditional or subsistence crops that are less profitable than cash crops does not necessarily reflect indifference to economic returns. Farming is inherently risky because the individual farmer has no control over his economic or physical environment. The farmer tries to reduce his risks by the judicious selection of enterprises, by crop diversification, and by spreading production over the growing season. As Upton's research in Africa indicates:

> Most individuals are risk avoiders, which means that they will choose less risky activities even though they may not be the most profitable on average over a period of years. Growing traditional crops for home consumption as well as the cash crops may provide protection against

2. Raj Krishna, "Agricultural Price Policy and Economic Development," in *Agricultural Development and Economic Growth*, ed. M. H. Southworth and B. F. Johnston (New York: Cornell University Press, 1967), pp. 497–540.

various risks: risks of failure of the cash crop, or of falling prices for it or of rising prices for the staple food crop in the local markets. Many farmers would maximize their average profits by growing only cash crops, but they maximize their satisfaction by avoiding risks.[3]

The farmer's behavior must be examined in relation to the set of circumstances within which he operates. Family relationships, the size of farms, the degree of fragmentation, the distance from markets, transport facilities, sources of information, channels of communication, the market structure, and uncontrollable production conditions are some of the influences that inhibit a more positive response to economic stimuli. For all practical purposes, as long as an individual invests his time, effort, or capital resources in combining inputs to create output, he is engaged in a business intended to produce an income.

The Term "Income"

The term "income" is often used interchangeably with revenue, receipts, sales, earnings, benefit, and profit. But each of these words has a different connotation. Various definitions have been offered for the term "farm income." It has been interpreted as (a) the gross value of all goods produced on the farm, whether sold for cash or not; (b) cash received from the sale of goods produced on the farm; (c) the net receipts from sales of produce after the advances for inputs such as feed, seed, and fertilizer are deducted; (d) the profit for an enterprise; and (e) the profit for the farm as a whole. The use of a single expression with different possible interpretations leads to confusion, because the context does not always give a clue to the intended meaning.

In this chapter several terms representing various elements of farm income are discussed. The expression "farm income" itself will refer generally to the profitability of the farm as a whole.

Analyzing Farm Enterprises

For the purpose of this study, the farm is considered as a firm having one or more enterprises. Enterprises are defined as the different subdivisions of the farm, each usually devoted to producing one kind of crop or live-

---

3. Upton, *Farm Management in Africa*, p. 8.

stock. A farm might consist of a single enterprise or several enterprises. One interesting phenomenon of small farms is mixed cropping, in which several crops are grown at the same time on the same parcel of land in such an intricate combination that it is virtually impossible to isolate the area for each constituent crop. In such cases, each mixed cropping combination should, for practical purposes, be regarded as one enterprise.

Enterprise studies are important in farm income analysis, because they help to explain the internal structure of the farm as a whole and to show the relative contribution of each enterprise to the whole organization. Sometimes the farm as a whole might be making a good profit, but one of its enterprises might be doing rather badly. Enterprise studies will (a) examine the relation between individual enterprises on a farm and their relation to the farm as a whole; (b) assess the profitability of each enterprise relative to the resources used; (c) compare the relative efficiency of various enterprises on the farm; (d) compare the efficiency of enterprises on various farms similar in type, size, and farming conditions; and (e) provide a basis for making rational decisions about the kind and size of enterprise, for calculating the costs of production, and for fixing the price of farm produce.

Enterprise studies are carried out easily if farm accounts are kept. Where these are not available, the essential data can be extracted from the standard financial accounts supplemented by physical records, the farm diary, and other data avalilable on the farm. Real problems arise, however, where the farmer, particularly on small farms, does not keep proper records of transactions on the farm. Under these circumstances it is still possible to analyze the enterprise, but the reliability of the study will depend on the memory of the farmer and on the skill of the analyst in eliciting the data and in removing possible biases.

In the typical small farm operation, family labor is usually the main input. Cash expenditure is generally quite low and is confined to cash crops. Usually it is possible to trace the quantity and value of inputs and outputs for most cash crop production. Quite often a marketing board, cooperative, or some other marketing agency finances the crop, buys the output, recovers the loan, and remits the balance to the farmer. In such cases there are account statements showing the quantity and value of each item of input and output. If the farmer finances a seasonal crop from his own resources, expenditure on inputs might be concentrated at the beginning of the season and income from output at the end.

When some of the produce is consumed on the farm, the revenue from sales understates production, and the value of farm output consumed on the farm must be estimated and added to the revenue from sales. Adjustment must be made for intermediate products, however.

Each enterprise usually produces a final output either for sale or for direct consumption by the farm family. The output of such enterprises is readily indentifiable, and its contribution to the profitability of the farm is easily assessed. Problems arise with intermediate products, such as pasture crops or feed grains, that are used as inputs for a further stage of the production process on the farm. The intermediate product may be treated either as a separate enterprise or as an integral part of the enterprise that uses it as an input.

Sometimes it may be useful to treat the intermediate product as a separate enterprise. Then the cost of producing it on the farm may be compared with the cost of purchasing a comparable product to find out whether it would be preferable to produce the commodity or to purchase it. The comparison may also indicate whether it would be better to sell the commodity in its intermediate stage than to use it as an input for an unprofitable enterprise on the farm. For example, a farmer may be an efficient producer of forage, but a poor manager of livestock, and the overall livestock enterprise may show a profit, because efficient forage production is subsidizing inefficient livestock husbandry. If a market exists for the fodder and grain produced, profits may be enhanced by concentrating on fodder production and discontinuing the livestock.

Enterprise income may be assessed by four different measures: gross output, net output, gross margin, and profit.

Farm enterprise gross output

The gross output is a preliminary measure of income. It assesses the performance of an enterprise purely in terms of the benefits it yields without considering the costs to produce them. The gross output of an enterprise is calculated by multiplying the total volume of the final marketable production by its average farm gate price. Final production normally excludes intermediate products. The total volume of production can be calculated either by multiplying the total area devoted to the crop by the average yield per unit area of marketable produce (excluding intermediate produce) or by aggregating the total amount of produce consumed on the farm and in the home, sold, fed to labor, or given away.

When comparing the gross outputs for the individual enterprises on the farm, the value of intermediate products would be included in the gross output. But in calculating the total gross output for all the enterprises on the farm, the value of intermediate products must be excluded to avoid double counting.

Generally, the farm gate represents the point of first sale. It marks the dividing line between income derived purely from production and income from marketing the produce. Thus, it would be incorrect to calculate the

Table 2–1. *Gross Output of Cabbage Production for One Year*

Item	First crop	Second crop	Average	Total
Acreage	3	2	—	5
Yield per acre (tons)	6	5	5.6	—
Production (tons)	18	10	—	28
Farm gate price per ton (dollars)	160	200	174	—
Gross output (dollars)	2,880	2,000	—	4,880
Gross output per acre (dollars)	960	1,000	976	

— Not applicable.
Source: Adapted from data prepared by the Agricultural Planning Unit, Ministry of Agriculture, Jamaica.

gross output for the enterprise by using the retail price at which the farmer sold the produce in the village marketplace or elsewhere off the farm. In those cases, marketing costs and marketing margins should be deducted from the gross output calculated at retail prices to arrive at the gross output at the farm gate price. The farm gate price is a weighted average that accounts for the variation of prices according to the grade of produce, the time of sale, and the market outlet. It is used to value both marketable produce and by-products that are not sold but consumed in the home, fed to labor, given away, or used as feed and seed.

Since it is possible to produce more than one short-term crop within a year, a distinction should be made between gross output for a particular season and gross output for the year. Table 2–1 shows how the gross output of a short-term crop is calculated for the year. The area for each crop is multiplied by the average yield to obtain the volume of production, which is then multiplied by the average farm gate price to derive the gross output for that crop. The gross output of cabbage for the year is the sum of the gross output for the two crops produced during the year. The gross output per acre for the year is derived by dividing the total gross output for the year by the total acreage of cabbage grown during the year.

Where stocks are carried over from one production period to another, such as in livestock production, gross output may be defined more precisely as the difference between the closing valuation of stocks plus sales (including marketable produce and by-products consumed on the farm or given away) and the opening valuation of stocks plus purchases.[4] Table 2–2 provides a simple hypothetical example of how gross output for a livestock enterprise is calculated. In this example the farmer fattens steers

4. United Kingdom Ministry of Agriculture, Fisheries, and Food, *The Farm as a Business* (London: Her Majesty's Stationery Office, 1958), p. 13.

Table 2–2. *Gross Output of Cattle Enterprise for One Year*

Item	Number and kind of cattle	Cost (dollars)			Total (dollars)
Closing valuation (at end of year)	15 steers @	240	=	3,600	
plus Sales (during the year)	10 steers @	280	=	2,800	6,400
minus Opening valuation (at beginning of year)	10 calves @	200	=	2,000	
plus Purchase (during the year)	15 calves @	140	=	2,100	4,100
Gross output (dollars)					$2,300
Acreage					15
Gross output per acre (dollars)					$ 153

on fifteen acres of improved pasture. He purchases calves weighing about 350 pounds each and costing about $40 per 100 pounds liveweight. He sells the fattened animals weighing about 800 pounds each at the average price of $35 per 100 pounds liveweight. He starts the year with ten calves, which he fattens and sells during the year, and he purchases another fifteen calves which remain in the herd at the end of the year.

In a more complex situation, the farmer could be involved in breeding as well as in fattening. The method of calculating the gross output would be the same as before. At the end of each year the farmer would make an inventory of the herd and value each category of animals according to the prevailing prices. The closing valuation for one year would be the opening valuation for the next.

The same principle is used to calculate the gross output for a dairy enterprise, but the value of milk produced would be added to the gross output of the cattle.

In farm management analysis, gross output is often expressed in relation to either the quantity or value of some critical input. Ratios commonly used are gross output per acre or gross output per dollar (or other unit of currency) of total cost, labor, fertilizer, or fuel. When expressed in such terms, gross output provides a preliminary basis for comparing the relative efficiency of an enterprise with that of other enterprises on the farm or on other similarly organized farms.

Farm enterprise net output

Enterprise net output is derived by subtracting the value of purchased feed and seed from the gross output of the enterprise.[5] This measure of

5. Ibid., p. 20

Table 2–3. *Gross Margin of Cabbage Production for One Year*

Item	First crop		Second crop		Total	
Gross output (dollars)		2,880		2,000		4,800
Variable costs (dollars)[a]						
Seed	15		10		25	
Fertilizer	318		212		530	
Fungicide	72		48		120	
Insecticide	45		30		75	
Gas and oil	150	600	100	400	250	1,000
Gross margin (dollars)		2,280		1,600		3,880
Acreage		3		2		5
Gross margin per acre (dollars)		760		800		776

a. Labor was not a variable cost in this example.
Source: Same as for Table 2–1.

enterprise income is particularly significant for livestock enterprises where purchased feed can be substituted for home-grown feed. The net output provides a basis for comparing the use of land on livestock farms with different feeding policies. For example, a farm relying heavily on purchased feed might reflect a more impressive level of gross output than a similar farm relying more on its own feed production. Purchasing feed is virtually equivalent to increasing the area of land devoted to feed production. Net output therefore provides a better measure for comparing the productive capacity of land devoted to livestock production than the gross output.

Farm enterprise gross margin

Costs can be conveniently divided into two main groups: variable and fixed costs. The enterprise gross margin is obtained by subtracting the variable costs from the gross output of the enterprise,[6] as illustrated in Table 2–3. Variable costs rise and fall with the size of the output and with the level of operation. Variable costs for items, such as feed, seed, fertilizer, spray materials, and casual labor, can be controlled to some extent, and are not incurred when there is no production. Fixed costs, for items such as taxes, insurance, interest, regular labor, and depreciation on build-

6. Clifford Selly and David Wallace, *Planning for Profit* (Farm Economics Branch, School of Agriculture, University of Cambridge, 1961), p. 4.

Table 2–4. *Labor Required to Produce an Acre of Cabbage for One Crop* (man-days)

Operations	August	September	October	November	December	January	Total
Land clearing	5	...	...	...	...	...	5
Ploughing and harrowing	40	...	...	...	...	...	40
Drilling holes and refining	...	26	...	...	...	...	26
Dropping seeds	...	7	...	...	...	...	7
Fertilizing	...	3	...	...	9	...	12
Weeding and moulding	...	...	20	15	15	...	50
Spraying	...	...	4	4	2	...	10
Reaping, cleaning, and packing	...	...	...	...	7	7	14
Transporting	...	...	...	...	...	...	...
Total	45	36	24	19	33	7	164

... Zero or negligible.
Source: Same as for Table 2–1.

ings and machines, are incurred whether or not there is production. The concept of gross margin is particularly useful in partial budgeting and linear programming analyses.

Farm enterprise profit

Enterprise profit is obtained by substracting the estimated total cost of production for the enterprise from its gross output. When the enterprise gross margin was calculated above, the variable costs were taken into account, but not fixed costs. Now, in calculating the enterprise profit, the total cost of production—fixed as well as variable—must be considered. For this purpose costs can be roughly divided into three categories: labor, materials, and other charges. Tables 2–4 and 2–5 illustrate the process of calculating the total cost of production. Enterprise profit is calculated by subtracting the total cost of production from the gross output, as shown below for the first crop of cabbage in Table 2–1:

Item	Amount
Yield per acre	6 tons
Farm gate price	$160/ton
Gross output per acre	$960
Total cost of production	$819
Enterprise profit per acre	$141

Labor required on the farm can be either supplied by the farm family or hired. Family labor does not constitute a cost in conventional account-

Table 2–5. *Total Cost to Produce an Acre of Cabbage for One Crop*

Item	Rate and quantity	Estimated cost (dollars)	Total (dollars)
(a) Labor operations			
Land clearing	$2.00/square for 10 squares[a,b]	20	
Ploughing and harrowing	$6.00/square for 10 squares[b]	60	
Drilling holes and refining	$3.50/day for 26 days	91	
Dropping seeds	$3.50/day for 7 days	24	
Fertilizing	$3.50/day for 12 days	42	
Weeding and moulding	$3.50/day for 50 days	175	
Spraying	$3.50/day for 10 days	35	
Reaping, cleaning, and packing	$3.50/day for 14 days	49	
Transportation	...	30	526
(b) Materials			
Seed	$4.00/pound for 1 pound	4	
Fertilizer	$6.60/bag for 16 bags	106	
Fungicide	$1.20/pound for 20 pounds	24	
Insecticide	$2.00/pound for 15 pounds	30	
Gas and oil	$5.00/week for 10 weeks	50	214
(c) Other charges			
Contingencies	5 percent of (a) + (b)	37	
Land charges	$20/acre annually	20	
Interest	6 percent of (a) + (b) semiannually	22	79
Total			819

... Zero or negligible.
a. 1 acre = 10 squares.
b. Land clearing, ploughing, and harrowing are compensated on the basis of the amount of land worked.

ing systems. But to estimate all possible costs in calculating the profit for each enterprise, labor is treated as though it were all hired.

The total cost of labor can be estimated in two different ways. The first simply adds the imputed cost of family labor to the actual cost of hired labor. The second method estimates the time required for all operations (Table 2–4) and then multiplies the result by the wage rate in the area (Table 2–5). The amount of labor required to perform similar operations on different farms may vary because of differences in the quality of labor, the level of skill and experience, and the incentives offered. For the purpose of calculating the cost of production and the enterprise profit, however, it is sufficient to use the average labor requirements on farms of similar type and size, operating under roughly similar conditions. (Labor budgets are discussed more fully in Chapter 5 in connection with their treatment in agricultural project analysis.)

The cost of materials is the easiest to handle. It generally constitutes the variable costs, which are easily identified. As shown in Table 2–5, the cost of materials is derived by multiplying the quantities required by the unit price of each item.

Other charges include such items as depreciation, rent, taxes, interest, physical contingencies, and other indirect costs. The cost of production for an enterprise does not include in full the purchase price of assets that last longer than one production period. Instead, the value of that portion of the asset used up for the enterprise is estimated and reflected as a charge for depreciation. Depreciation may be calculated by several methods, the more popular being the straight-line and the diminishing-balance. In the straight-line method, the estimated total depreciation—the purchase price minus the scrap value—is distributed evenly over the expected life of the asset, and a constant amount is written off each year. In the diminishing-balance method a constant percentage is written off, and the annual amount of depreciation decreases each year. In calculating the portion of annual deprecation that can be allocated to an enterprise, the usage, the cropping period, the percentage of the total farm area devoted to the enterprise, or other relevant factors are considered.

Rent and land taxes are apportioned according to the area of the farm devoted to the enterprise and to the duration of the crop. Where the land is owned, a rental value is imputed at the current rental rate for similar land. In this way, all costs are taken into consideration, and the enterprise may be compared with other farms where the land is rented.

The cost of physical contingencies is provided in case miscellaneous items are overlooked. It is an arbitrary figure usually estimated at from 5 to 10 percent of the cost of materials and labor.

Interest is usually defined as the payment for the use of borrowed capital. Since the capital requirements of the farm may be supplied partly by the farmer and partly by outside sources, it is usually difficult to determine how much interest should be included in the cost. How interest should be treated also depends on the different purposes of a farm income analysis:

(a) If the purpose is to obtain the cost of production for an enterprise, interest should be imputed at market rate for all costs incurred for the enterprise as though all the money required to produce the crop were borrowed;

(b) If the purpose is to obtain the net farm income (discussed later in this chapter), only the interest actually paid on borrowed capital should be included in the cost;

The enterprise profit only partially reflects the benefit accruing to the farm family. The farm also provides the family with employment. Large and complex farms may rely heavily on hired labor, but on small farms the family contributes the bulk of the labor required. In calculating the enterprise profit for an acre of cabbage in Table 2–5, it was assumed that all labor was hired. But if the farm family actually performed the following functions, they would retain $381 as compensation for their labor:

Labor operation	Estimated cost (dollars)
Drilling holes and refining	91
Dropping seeds	24
Fertilizing	42
Weeding and moulding	175
Reaping, cleaning, and packing	49
Total	381

Thus, the total amount accruing to the farm family from the cabbage enterprise would be the sum of the enterprise profit and the compensation for the family labor: that is, $141 + $381, a total of $522 per acre.

Farm family labor helps small farms to survive in periods of falling prices. For instance, if the calculations of farm enterprise profit were based on the assumption that the farm gate price was $120 per ton instead of $160 per ton, the gross output would be $720 instead of $960, and there would be a loss of $99 instead of a profit of $141. To the farmer, however, it would mean that he is getting $282: that is, $99 less than the $381 calculated for family labor. In other words, family labor would be compensated at a rate less than the normal wage rate. Some farmers may then decide to change their cropping programs or to go out of production, whereas others may accept this low rate and continue to produce in hopes of a better price in the future. The farmer's reaction may be determined by the availability of alternative sources of income, the reservation price for his labor,[7] and expectations for the future.

---

7. The reservation price is the rate below which the farmer would prefer to withhold his labor rather than to accept employment.

Net Farm Income

Net farm income is the principal measure of the year-by-year profitability of the farm as a whole. It is the reward for the labor, capital, and management contributed by the farm family during the year. In some developed countries the farm family is defined as the farmer and his wife;[8] work done by other members of the family is treated as hired labor. But this definition is not consistent with the cultural patterns in many developing countries, where the farm family will include all the members of the household who normally live on the farm, who contribute their labor and other resources to operate the farm, and who share in the benefits from the farm.

The net farm income is obtained by subtracting the total cost for all enterprises, except the imputed values for farm family labor and capital, from the total gross output of all the enterprises. In calculating the items of cost, as in calculating the gross output, adjustment has to be made for the opening and closing valuation of stocks on hand. This adjustment particularly affects items that are sometimes bought in bulk, with stocks carried over from one year to the next, such as feed, seed, fertilizer, chemicals, and fuel.

In computing the net farm income, the cost for the purchase of assets that have a productive life of more than one year is considered relative to their annual value of depreciation. This value is determined by the cost of the item, the life of the asset, and the method of calculating depreciation. The value of marketable by-products is included in the gross output for each enterprise. Subsidies and crop bonuses should be reflected in the gross output for the appropriate enterprise, or should be added to the total gross output if it is difficult to allocate them to the respective enterprises. Loans are not included in the gross output, just as the repayment of loans is not included as a cost. The total cost also includes interest paid on borrowed capital, but not the return on capital invested by the farm family or the compensation for family labor.

Tables 2–6, 2–7, and 2–8, illustrate the calculation of the net farm income for a five-acre irrigated farm, based on a model proposed for the Hounslow Irrigation Scheme in Jamaica.[9] The crop production program for the farm is outlined in Table 2–6. The cropping intensity, which is

8. United Kingdom Ministry of Agriculture, *The Farm as a Business*, p. 11.
9. Economic Development Institute, "The Appraisal of the Hounslow Irrigation Scheme," prepared by participants in the Agricultural Projects Course (Washington, D.C.: World Bank, 1973; processed).

Table 2–6. *Cropping Program*

| | Crop calendar | | |
Item	Planting	Harvesting	Acreage
Peanut	January	April	1.8
Corn	January	June	0.9
Sweet potato	January	August	1.8
Corn	April	October	0.9
Lettuce	April	August	0.9
Tomato	June	October	0.9
Tomato	August	December	0.9
Red peas	August	December	1.8
Peanut	October	December	1.8
Total acreage			11.7
Size of farm (acres)			5.0
Cropping intensity (percent)			230

Source: Adapted from data in Economic Development Institute, "The Appraisal of the Hounslow Irrigation Scheme."

derived by dividing the total area cropped by the size of the farm, is 230 percent. The farm is divided into three plots. The cropping sequence for these plots is given in Table 2–7.

Table 2–8 shows that the net farm income $2,470 is obtained by subtracting the total of variable cost ($1,494) and overhead cost ($750) from the total gross output of all the enterprises ($4,714). The net farm income represents the compensation to the farm family for their labor, capital investment, and management of the farm.

Family labor income is the imputed value of the manual labor contributed by the farm family. This imputed value is based on the rate that the farmer would have to pay for hired labor. In the model in Table 2–8, the labor of the farm family is valued at the same rate of $3.50 per day paid for hired labor.

When the net farm income is equal to the family labor income, the farm is just able to pay for family labor, with nothing left for management or return on investment. When the net farm income is less than the family labor income, the farm family would be compensated for their labor at a wage rate lower than what they could earn if they were employed as laborers on some other farm. In this example, the net farm income is $2,470, giving a surplus of $895 after deducting the family labor income.

The surplus represents the compensation for the management and the capital contributed by the family. Investment income is subtracted next,

Table 2–7. *Cropping Sequence*

Month	Plot 1 (1.8 acres)		Plot 2 (0.9 acres)	Plot 3 (1.8 acres)
January	Peanut		Corn	Sweet potato
April	Corn	Lettuce		
June			Tomato	
August		Tomato		Red pea
October	Peanut		Peanut	
December				

Source: Same as for Table 2–7.

and the residual is the management income. Investment income is calculated by imputing the same rate of interest for the family's capital as the rate of interest paid on loans. Management income is the profit from the farm as a whole accruing to the farm family for taking risks and performing the managerial function.

To summarize the relation between the enterprise profit and the net farm income, farm income analysis can be divided into enterprise income analysis and net farm income analysis. Enterprise income analysis shows the profitability of each individual enterprise. Net farm income analysis is used to calculate the profitability of the farm as a whole. In calculating the enterprise profit, the imputed costs of family labor and capital are included in the total cost and are deducted from the gross output for each enterprise. But in calculating the net farm income, the imputed costs of family labor and capital are not included in the total cost. It is only after

Table 2–8. *Net Farm Income, Family Labor Income, and Management and Investment Income*

Item	Peanut	Corn	Lettuce	Tomato	Red pea	Sweet potato	Total
Area cropped (acres)	3.6	1.8	0.9	1.8	1.8	1.8	11.7
Yield per acre (ton)	0.6	1.4	4.8	6.0	0.92	6.0	—
Production (ton)	2.16	2.52	4.32	10.8	1.66	10.8	—
Price per ton (dollars)	400	150	150	140	400	60	—
Gross output	864	378	648	1,512	664	648	4,714
Variable costs							
Seed	144	20	22	20	68	—	
Fertilizer	150	65	63	130	50	46	
Chemicals	30	25	18	240	32	—	
Stakes	—	—	—	130	—	—	
Custom work	54	15	42	112	18	—	
Total	378	125	145	632	168	46	1,494
Gross margin	486	253	503	880	496	602	3,220
Overhead costs							
Rent: 5 acres at $20 per acre						100	
Hired labor: 100 days at $3.50 per day						350	
Other charges: Depreciation, interest, repair, fuel, and so forth						300	750
Net farm income							2,470
Family labor income							
Farmer: 300 days at $3.50						1,050	
Wife: 150 days at $3.50						525	
Total							1,575
Management and investment income							895

— Not applicable.
Source: Same as for Table 2–7.

the net farm income is calculated that the imputed costs of family labor and capital are deducted; the residual is the management income. The management income for the farm is equal to the total of the profits from all enterprises.

3

•—•—•—•—•—•—•—•—•—•—•—••—•

Partial and Break-even Budgets

Enterprise analysis is essential for the proper management of the farm. It helps to explain the internal structure of the farm by showing the relative contribution of each enterprise to the farm as a whole. The farm manager can use the analysis to prepare budgets that help him make better decisions on which enterprises to expand, reduce, or eliminate; which new enterprises to introduce; and what adjustments to make in the organization.

Basically there are two types of budgeting: complete budgeting and partial budgeting.[1] The former is appropriate for a massive reorganization of the farm; the latter, for relatively minor adjustments. Another kind of budget, referred to as the break-even budget, is really a type of partial budget.

Partial Budgets

The partial budget, the simplest form of budgetary analysis, commonly is used in estimating the profitability of relatively minor changes in an existing organization. It is a form of marginal analysis designed to show, not profit or loss for the farm as a whole, but the net increase or decrease in net farm income resulting from the proposed changes.

Generally, partial budgets consider four basic items classified as follows:

Costs	Benefits
(a) New costs	(c) Costs saved
(b) Revenue foregone	(d) New revenue

1. United Kingdom, Ministry of Agriculture, Fisheries and Food, *The Farm as a Business* (London: Her Majesty's Stationery Office, 1958), p. 52.

The difference between (a) + (b) and (c) + (d) will indicate whether the change is profitable. If (c) + (d) exceeds (a) + (b), the proposed change would increase farm income, provided that it is technically feasible.

Partial budgets can be used when considering whether or not to introduce new inputs, enterprises, or farm practices; to substitute an input or enterprise; or to change farm practices or marketing arrangements. Partial budgeting is simplest when a new input, farm practice, or enterprise is introduced. For example, a farmer may wish to test the profitability of introducing fertilizers or crop spraying. Or he would like to find out whether it is feasible to add a supplementary enterprise, such as poultry or pig rearing to utilize the surplus labor on the farm. In this case there would not be any cost saved or revenue foregone. Whether a new enterprise is justifiable depends on whether it is technically feasible and whether the new revenue earned exceeds the new cost incurred.

Technical feasibility is an essential precondition for partial budgeting, since it is useless to test the economic feasibility of a program which cannot be implemented or for which the technical assumptions are not valid. To say that a program is technically feasible means that the soil, climate, and other physical and biological factors are conducive to the proper growth of the crops or livestock under consideration. It also means that the management can introduce the change without undue strain on the existing organization.

Table 3–1 presents a simple illustration of a partial budget. The objective of the budget is to test the profitability of substituting the Sebago variety of Irish potato with the Arran Consul variety. The basic assumptions are as follows:

(a) Seeding rate—1,500 pounds per acre for each variety.
(b) Price of seed—Sebago, $6.50 per 100 pounds
                   —Arran Consul, $7.00 per 100 pounds
(c) Land—land is rented for the duration of each crop.
(d) Labor—labor is all hired.
(e) Capital—the farmer provides all the capital.
(f) Crop period—Sebago, 10 weeks
                 —Arran Consul, 14 weeks
(g) Yield per acre—Sebago, 7,500 pound per acre
                   —Arran Consul, 10,500 pound per acre
(h) Price of table potato—Sebago, $8.00 per 100 pounds
                          —Arran Consul, $8.00 per 100 pounds
(i) Management—the change is technically feasible and will not impose undue strain on the existing organization.

The new costs include all the direct and indirect costs incurred in

Table 3–1. *Partial Budget for Substituting One Acre of Sebago with Arran Consul Potatoes*
(dollars)

Costs			Benefits		
(a) *New costs*			(c) *Costs saved*		
Arran Consul seed	105		Sebago seed		98
Spray materials	16				
Labor	40				
Rent	12	173			
(b) *Revenue foregone*			(d) *New revenue*		
Gross output of Sebago table potatoes		600	Gross output of Arran Consul table potatoes		840
		773			938
Additional profit per acre from Arran Consul potato		165			
		938			

Source: Adapted from data prepared by the Agricultural Planning Unit, Ministry of Agriculture, Jamaica.

producing the new variety of potatoes. For instance, Arran Consul seed is a new cost because this particular variety was not produced before. New costs in this case also include: (a) the cost of additional chemicals required to spray the crop for four more weeks; (b) the cost of labor for spraying for four more weeks and harvesting an additional 3,000 pounds of potatoes; and (c) the additional rent for the land for four more weeks. The cost saved, $98, is the amount that would have been spent on the Sebago seed. In the case where the substitute is an entirely different crop, all the variable costs for growing the original crop would be treated as costs saved. In this example, only the variety is changed. It is assumed that apart from the cost of the seed, the expenses for cultivating both varieties are the same up to the tenth week. The revenue foregone is the gross output of $600 that would be earned if the production of the Sebago variety were not discontinued. The new revenue is the gross output expected from the Arran Consul variety of table potatoes.

The partial budget in Table 3–1 shows that the Arran Consul variety of potatoes will yield an additional profit of $165 for each acre of the Sebago variety that it replaces. It tells only the amount of the additional profit expected from the change, but not the total profit for the farm if the change is made.

The items to be included in a partial budget vary according to the particular circumstances in each case. In the example above, land was included because rent was assumed to be a variable cost. In the case presented in Table 3–2, the land is assumed to be either owned by the farmer or rented on a long-term basis, and hence, the rent becomes a fixed or overhead cost. Labor may also be treated differently. In Table 3–1 labor is assumed to be all hired and therefore constitutes a variable cost; in Table 3–2 labor is a fixed cost, because the farm family presumably supplies all the labor, and therefore the cost of labor will not vary regardless of the level of production.

The partial budget in Table 3–2 tests the profitability of substituting peanuts with red peas. The basic assumptions are as follows:

(a) Land—the land is owned by the farmer.
(b) Labor—labor is all supplied by the farm family, and there are no alternative employment opportunities outside the farm during the production period.
(c) Management—the change is technically feasible. Red peas are a perfect substitute for peanuts in the crop rotation. The change will not impose undue strain on the existing organization of the farm.

In this example the new costs include all the variable costs for producing red peas. The costs saved are the variable costs for growing peanuts. Land and labor are treated as fixed costs and are not included in the budget. The case would be different, however, if red peas required a longer production period than peanuts, disrupted the rotation program, and led to the sacrifice of the crop that would normally follow the peanuts. Then

Table 3–2. *Partial Budget for Substituting One Acre of Peanuts with Red Peas*
(dollars)

Costs			Benefits		
(a) *New costs*: Variable costs for growing red peas			(c) *Costs saved*: Variable costs for growing peanuts		
Seed	50		Seed	40	
Fertilizer	30		Fertilizer	40	
Chemicals	30	110	Chemicals	10	90
(b) *Revenue foregone*			(d) *New revenue*		
Gross output of peanuts		240	Gross output of red peas		370
		350			460
Additional profit per acre from red peas		110			
		460			

Source: Same as for Table 3–1.

the profit normally earned from the succeeding crop would have to be included in the revenue foregone.

The partial budget in Table 3–2 shows that substituting peanuts with red peas would increase profit by $110 an acre. The amount of additional profit may be calculated in either of two ways:

$$(costs\ saved\ +\ new\ revenue)\ -\ (new\ costs\ +\ revenue\ foregone)$$
$$=\ \$(90\ +\ 370)\ -\ (110\ +\ 240)\ =\ \$110.$$

or

$$(new\ revenue\ -\ new\ costs)\ -\ (revenue\ foregone\ -\ costs\ saved)$$
$$=\ \$(370\ -\ 110)\ -\ (240\ -\ 90)\ =\ \$110.$$

The second method makes use of the gross margin, obtained by subtracting variable costs from gross output. Subtracting the new costs (variable costs for red peas) from the new revenue (the gross output of red peas)

Table 3–3. *Break-even Budget for Substituting Sebago with Arran Consul Potatoes*
(dollars)

Item		Cost or Benefit
Sebago Irish potatoes		
Gross output		
Sale of 7,500 pounds of table potatoes at $8.00 per 100 pounds		600
Variable costs		
Hired labor	240	
Seed	98	
Fertilizer and spray materials	115	
Rent	30	483
Gross margin		117
Arran Consul Irish potatoes		
Variable costs		
Hired labor	280	
Seed	105	
Fertilizer and spray materials	131	
Rent	42	558
Gross margin from Sebago potatoes		117
Minimum return that must be obtained from Arran Consul potatoes		675
Price per 100 pounds for table potatoes = 8.00		
Break-even yield for Arran Consul potatoes = 675 ÷ 8 = 8,438 pounds per acre		

Source: Same as for Table 3–1.

gives the gross margin for red peas; subtracting the costs saved (variable costs for peanuts) from the revenue foregone (gross output of peanuts) gives the gross margin for peanuts. Then, subtracting the gross margin for peanuts from the gross margin for red peas gives the additional profit gained in substituting one crop for the other.

Break-even Budgets

The purpose of a break-even budget is to estimate the maximum acceptable level of an item of cost given an estimated level of benefit, or the minimum acceptable level of an item of benefit given an estimated level of cost. In preparing a partial budget the values of all the variables are known. In preparing a break-even budget the value of an important variable is unknown, and the purpose of the budget is to calculate the break-even value of that variable. For example, a farmer might be interested in substituting one variety of a crop with another, but the productive potential of the new variety is unknown. In this case, the break-even budget could indicate the minimum yield that would have to be achieved to make the change worthwhile. Or, if the expected yield is known but the price is not, the break-even budget could indicate the minimum price that must be obtained to make the change economically feasible.

The preparation of a break-even budget is illustrated in Table 3–3. The assumptions are exactly the same as those for Table 3–1, except that in this case, Arran Consul is supposed to be the new variety, and its yield is not known. The purpose of the budget is to calculate the break-even yield, or the minimum yield that must be obtained for the Arran Consul variety in order to maintain at least the $117 per acre gross margin produced by the Sebago variety.

The analysis in Table 3–3 shows that the break-even yield for the Arran Consul variety is 8,438 pounds per acre. If the farmer estimates the average yield to be 10,000 pounds per acre, but he is not sure about the price of the new variety, the minimum return of $675 may be divided by 10,000 pounds to obtain a break-even price of $6.75 per 100 pounds. To this price should be added an additional amount to compensate the farmer for taking the risk of making the change. The amount of this compensation depends upon the farmer, the incentives offered, and the confidence he has in surpassing the break-even yield.

4

●━●

Transition to
Complete Budgeting and
Agricultural Project Analysis

Partial budgeting is appropriate when the proposed change will have a relatively minor effect on the farm organization, or will produce benefits within a relatively short period, say, a year. When the proposed change will have a long-term effect, as in a comprehensive reorganization of a farm, complete budgeting must be undertaken.

The methodology of complete budgeting overlaps with that used in project analysis. Complete budgeting is normally associated with the analysis of a single farm, whereas agricultural project analysis is associated with many farms, but this is a false distinction. An agricultural project may consist of a single farm or many farms. It may also consist of one or more enterprises on a single farm or on a number of farms.

An agricultural project may be defined simply as a specific investment activity on a single farm or on a large number of farms, in which resources are used over a short period with the expectation of a greater flow of benefits to be realized over an extended period in the future. Projects have specific beginning and terminating dates. They are geared to benefit particular interest groups, generally (although not necessarily) in a particular location. In this chapter a few basic considerations which are important in the analysis of agricultural projects are discussed.

Time Value of Money and Discounting

In both the economic and financial analyses of an agricultural project, the changing value of money over time must be considered because subjective considerations as well as investment opportunities generally lead to a preference for present resources over future resources. Since the effect of reorganizing a farm or of implementing a project is usually distributed over several accounting periods, the time when costs and benefits occur determines how valuable they are. The bulk of the cost is usually incurred at the beginning of the project, and the benefits arise later. If the project extends over several accounting periods, the values of the cost and benefit streams must be standardized to provide a proper basis for comparison. This can be done by reducing the values to their "present worth," also referred to as present value or discounted value.

The process of calculating the present value of a sum of money due some time in the future is called discounting. It is the reverse of compounding. Compounding translates present cash flows into their future values; discounting calculates the present value of future cash flows. Compounding looks from the present into the future; discounting looks backward from the future to the present.

The rate for discounting is called the discount rate. The difference in the value of the same sum of money in two different periods is determined by the discount factor. This is affected by the length of time and by the discount rate used. At any given discount rate the value of a sum of money becomes less and less the further in the future it is to be received. For instance, $100 today is more valuable than $100 to be received one year later. Also the greater the discount rate, the greater the difference will be between the value of a sum of money in two different periods. Table 4–1(a), (b) and (c) illustrates the principle of compounding and discounting, assuming a rate of 10 percent.

In section (a), $683 is supposedly invested for four years at 10 percent compounded annually. At the end of the first year, the investment earns $68 interest, so that the total amount due is $751. If this amount of $751 is invested for the second year, the total due at the end of the second year is $826. By this process of compound growth, the original investment of $683 increases to $1,000 at the end of the fourth year.

This process is reversed in sections (b) and (c). If the amount of $1,000 is to be received at the end of the fourth year, how much must be invested now at an interest rate of 10 percent? In other words, what is the present worth of $1,000 due at the end of the fourth year at 10 percent rate of interest? Table 4–1(b) shows the process of discounting by completely reversing the calculations for compounding in (a). In compounding the investment at the beginning of each year is multiplied by (1 + the rate of interest) to obtain the amount due at the end of the year. In discounting, the amount due at the end of each year is divided by (1 + the rate of

Table 4–1. *Compounding and Discounting Principles*

(a) Compounding

Year	Investment (dollars)		Rate[a]		Amount due at end of year (dollars)
1	683	×	1.10	=	751
2	751	×	1.10	=	826
3	826	×	1.10	=	909
4	909	×	1.10	=	1,000

(b) Discounting—first example

Year	Amount due at end of year (dollars)		Rate		Worth at beginning of year (dollars)
4	1,000	÷	1.10	=	909
3	909	÷	1.10	=	826
2	826	÷	1.10	=	751
1	751	÷	1.10	=	683

(c) Discounting—second example

Year	Amount due at end of year (dollars)		Discount factor		Present worth (dollars)
4	1,000	×	0.909	=	909
3	909	×	0.909	=	826
2	826	×	0.909	=	751
1	751	×	0.909	=	683

a. The rate used is (1 + the rate of interest): that is, 1.00 for the recovery of principal and 0.10 for 10 percent interest.

interest) to obtain its value at the beginning of the year. Table 4–1(c) shows an alternative method of discounting. The amount due at the end of the year is multiplied by 0.909, which is the reciprocal of 1.10 and is the discount factor for one year at the rate of 10 percent.

Compounding and discounting tables have been prepared to facilitate these calculations.[1] Since most of these tables are intended primarily for project evaluation, the rate of interest is assumed to be an annual rate, and the intervals are referred to as years. Intervals other than years can be construed by modifying the annual rate of interest and by considering the "year" columns as "period" columns. For purposes of discounting, Git-

1. J. Price Gittinger (ed.), *Compounding and Discounting Tables for Project Evaluation* (Baltimore: Johns Hopkins University Press, 1973).

tinger assumes that both costs and benefits fall on the last day of each project year, including the first year, and so all costs and benefits in the first year are discounted as though they arose at the end of the year.[2]

The tables show the discount factors for each year at specific discount rates. Given the discount rate, the present worth of an amount due in any year in the future can be found by multiplying that amount by the discount factor shown in the tables for the corresponding year. For example, to find the present worth of $1,000 due four years later at a 10 percent rate, $1,000 is multiplied by 0.683, the discount factor for the fourth year. The result is $683.[3]

The tables can also be used to calculate the present worth of a constant amount to be received at regular intervals for a continuous period in the future at a given discount rate. The present worth of a constant sum of $200 to be received for 5 years from year 4 through year 8 at a discount rate of 10 percent may be calculated as follows:

Year	Amount (dollars)	Discount factor at 10 percent	Present worth at 10 percent (dollars)
4	200	0.683	136.6
5	200	0.621	124.2
6	200	0.564	112.8
7	200	0.513	102.6
8	200	0.467	93.4
Total		2.848	569.6

The total present worth, $569.60, is obtained by adding together the present worths of $200 each year. But the same result may be obtained by adding together the discount factors for each year and multiplying the sum (2.848) by $200. The sum of discount factors is given as the present worth of an annuity factor in the compounding and discounting tables (see footnote 1). The present worth of an annuity factor can be considered as a running total of the discount factors. For instance the present worth of an annuity factor for the fifth year at a rate of 10 percent is 3.791, which is the sum of the discount factors for years 1 through 5. In the example used here, the constant stream of $200 does not start in year 1 but in year 4, and it ends in year 8. To find the present worth of an annuity factor from year 4 to 8, the factor for year 3 is subtracted from the factor for year 8, that is: 5.335 − 2.487 = 2.848. Thus, the same result is obtained as resulted from adding the discount factors for years 4 to 8.

2. Ibid, p. 129.
3. The discount factor is rounded to three places of decimal according to conventional rules.

Discounted Measures of Project Worth

Three important measures of project worth incorporate the principles of discounting: (a) benefit/cost ratio; (b) net present worth, also called net present value; and (c) internal rate of return.

Benefit/cost ratio

The benefit/cost ratio compares the present worths of the benefit and cost of a project and expresses their relation as a ratio. The discount rate used is usually the opportunity cost of capital.

Tables 4–2, 4–3, and 4–4 illustrate three common ways to calculate the benefit/cost ratio:

Method I.   Discounted gross benefits divided by the total discounted gross costs (including investment, operation and maintenance, and production costs);

Method II.   Discounted gross benefits minus production costs, divided by the discounted total of investment, operation, and maintenance costs; and

Method III. The sum of the discounted net benefits in those years when gross benefit exceeds total cost (discounted positive net benefits) divided by the sum of discounted net benefits in those years when total costs exceed gross benefits (discounted negative net benefits).[4]

The tables show that the benefit/cost ratio is 1.39 if calculated by the first method, 1.8 by the second, and 2.77 by the third. This illustrates one of the problems with the benefit/cost ratio: the size of the ratio is affected by the method used to calculate it. Generally, any method that reduces the size of the denominator will increase the ratio.

If all the costs and benefits of a project are measurable, the benefit/cost ratio is a useful tool for determining whether to accept or to reject the project. The simple decision rule is to accept the project if the benefit/cost ratio is greater than one and to reject it if the ratio is less than one.

Net present worth

The net present worth is the difference between the present worths of the benefits and costs of a project. As in the case of the benefit/cost ratio,

4. Colin Bruce, "Social Cost-Benefit Analysis: A Guide for Country and Project Economists to the Derivation and Application of Economic and Social Accounting Prices," World Bank Staff Working Paper, no. 239 (Washington, D.C.: World Bank, 1976; processed).

Table 4–2. *Calculation of Benefit/Cost Ratio and Net Present Worth: Method I. Gross Benefits Compared with Gross Costs*
(thousands of Jamaican dollars)

Year	Investment costs (I)	Operation and maintenance costs (O+M)	Production costs (P)	Gross costs (I+O+M+P)	Gross benefits (B)	Discount factor at 12 percent	Present worth of gross costs at 12 percent	Present worth of gross benefits at 12 percent
1	1,324	—	208	1,532	765	0.893	1,368	683
2	1,650	—	208	1,858	765	0.797	1,481	610
3	1,348	141	251	1,740	820	0.712	1,239	584
4	—	239	440	679	1,785	0.636	432	1,135
5	—	239	444	683	1,973	0.567	387	1,119
6	—	239	444	683	1,912	0.507	346	969
7	—	208	910	1,118	2,070	0.452	506	936
8–15	—	208[a]	915[a]	1,123[a]	2,127[a]	2.247[d]	2,523	4,779
16	200	208	915	1,323	2,127	0.163	216	347
17–26	—	208[b]	915[b]	1,323[b]	2,127[b]	0.922[e]	1,036	1,961
27	200	208	915	1,323	2,127	0.047	62	100
28–38	—	208[c]	915[c]	1,123[c]	2,127[c]	0.278[f]	312	591
Total	4,722	7,514	31,270	43,506	76,027	8.221	9,908	13,814

Benefit/cost ratio at 12 percent = 13,814/9,908 = 1.39
Net present worth at 12 percent = J$13,814,000 − J$9,908,000 = J$3,906,000

— Not applicable.
a. Annual amount is included eight times in the total.
b. Annual amount is included ten times in the total.
c. Annual amount is included eleven times in the total.
d. The present worth of an annuity factor for years 8 to 15.
e. The present worth of annuity factor for years 17 to 26.
f. The present worth of an annuity factor for years 28 to 38.

Source: Adapted from Economic Development Institute, "Field Workshop Report; Appraisal of Meylersfield Drainage Project," prepared by participants in the Rural Development Course (Washington, D.C.: World Bank 1977; processed), Table 8–2.

the rate used for discounting is usually the opportunity cost of capital. The simple decision rule is to accept projects for which the net present worth is positive. Unlike the benefit/cost ratio, it is not affected by the different methods used in calculating it. Tables 4–2, 4–3, and 4–4 show that the net present worth remains the same (J$3,906,000) whichever method of computation is used. Being an absolute measure, the net present worth is not effective for comparing the profitability of alternative investments. It is an important complement to the internal rate of return, however, particularly in comparing projects that are mutually exclusive or that have rates of return over 50 percent. Chapter 8 deals with these cases in greater detail.

Internal rate of return

The internal rate of return is that rate at which the present worth of the cost is equal to the present worth of the benefit. At this rate the benefit/cost ratio is as close as possible to one, the net present worth is as close as possible to zero, and the sum of the positive net benefits is almost equal to the sum of the negative net benefits. The internal rate of return is usually found by trial and error, since there is no simple mathematical formula to facilitate the computation. A reasonable rate at which to discount costs and benefits would be selected to arrive at the net present worth. If at the rate the net present worth is positive, a higher discount rate would be tried; and if it is negative, a lower discount rate. Table 4–5 illustrates the process of the calculation. At the discount rate of 26 percent, the net present worth is J$339,000, which means that the discount rate is too low. At the higher rate of 31 percent, the net present worth is −J$48,000, which means that the discount rate is too high. The internal rate of return is therefore somewhere between 26 percent and 31 percent. It can then be found by interpolation according to the following formula:[5]

$$\begin{matrix} \text{Internal} \\ \text{rate} \\ \text{of return} \end{matrix} = \begin{matrix} \text{Lower} \\ \text{discount} \\ \text{rate} \end{matrix} + \begin{matrix} \text{Difference} \\ \text{between the two} \\ \text{discount rates} \end{matrix} \times \dfrac{\text{Net present worth at lower discount rate}}{\begin{matrix}\text{Sum of the two net present worths,} \\ \text{disregarding the signs}\end{matrix}}$$

As shown in Table 4–5, the net present worth at the lower rate of 26 percent has a positive value (J$339,000). At the higher rate of 31 percent the net present worth has a negative value (−J$48,000). The difference

5. J. Price Gittinger, *Economic Analysis of Agricultural Projects* (Baltimore: Johns Hopkins University Press, 1972), p. 80.

Table 4-3. Calculation of Benefit/Cost Ratio and Net Present Worth: Method II. (Gross Benefits – Production Costs) Compared with (Investment + Operation and Maintenance Costs) (thousands of Jamaican dollars)

Year	Investment costs (I)	Operation and maintenance costs (O+M)	(I) + (O + M)	Discount factor at 12 percent	Present worth of (I)+(O+M) at 12 percent	Gross benefits (B)	Production costs (P)	(B) – (P)	Discount factor at 12 percent	Present worth of (B) – (P) at 12 percent
1	1,324	—	1,324	0.893	1,182	765	208	557	0.893	497
2	1,650	—	1,650	0.797	1,315	765	208	557	0.797	444
3	1,348	141	1,489	0.712	1,060	820	251	569	0.712	405
4	—	239	239	0.636	152	1,785	440	1,345	0.636	855
5	—	239	239	0.567	135	1,973	444	1,529	0.567	867
6	—	239	239	0.507	121	1,912	444	1,468	0.507	744
7	—	208	208	0.452	94	2,070	910	1,160	0.452	524
8–15	—	208[a]	208[a]	2.247[d]	467	2,127[a]	915[a]	1,212[a]	2.247[d]	2,723
16	200	208	408	0.163	67	2,127	915	1,212	0.163	198
17–26	—	208[b]	208[b]	0.922[e]	192	2,127[b]	915[b]	1,212[b]	0.922[e]	1,117
27	200	208	408	0.047	19	2,127	915	1,212	0.047	57
28–38	—	208[c]	208[c]	0.278[f]	58	2,127[c]	915[c]	1,212[c]	0.278[f]	337
Total	4,722	7,514	12,236	8.221	4,862	76,027	31,270	44,757	8.221	8,768

Benefit/cost ratio at 12 percent = 8,768/4,862 = 1.80
Net present worth at 12 percent = J$8,768,000 – J$4,862,000 = J$3,906,000

— Not applicable.
a. Annual amount is included eight times in the total.
b. Annual amount is included ten times in the total.
c. Annual amount is included eleven times in the total.
Source: Same as for Table 4-2.

d. The present worth of an annuity factor for years 8 to 15.
e. The present worth of an annuity factor for years 17 to 26.
f. The present worth of an annuity factor for years 28 to 38.

between the two rates is 5 percent; the difference between the net present worths is J$387,000. Hence, the internal rate of return = 26 + 5 (339,000 ÷ 387,000) = 26 + 4.38 = 30.38, or 30 percent to the nearest round number.

Since the internal rate of return derived by interpolation is sometimes overstated, it should be checked by repeating the calculation for the net present worth at that rate, as shown in the last two columns in Table 4–5. If the internal rate of return is correctedly estimated, the result of that calculation should be close to zero. Because the rate of return is rounded to the nearest whole number, however, the net present worth is seldom exactly zero at that rate: that is, the present worth of the benefits is seldom exactly equal to the present worth of the costs at the interpolated internal rate of return.

One of the main criticisms of the internal rate of return is that the calculation is tedious. An explanation of how the process may be simplified has been developed by Schaefer-Kehnert. [6]

The internal rate of return has distinct advantages over other discounted measures of project worth. First, its calculation does not depend on assumptions about the opportunity cost of capital. Second, unlike the net present worth, it is a relative measure that can be used to compare the profitability of projects. The rate of return represents the average rate of interest at which a project pays back the investment over its lifetime. It therefore is a criterion for comparing alternative investment opportunities.

This study will use the internal rate of return as the principal measure of project worth. The World Bank also uses it to gauge the projects it finances. The internal rate of return calculated from a financial analysis is called the internal financial return or the financial rate of return, to distinguish it from the internal economic return or the economic rate of return calculated from an economic analysis.

The rate of return has certain limitations which apply equally to the financial and the economic analysis. These limitations are discussed in conjunction with economic analysis in Chapter 8.

The simple decision rule in this case for choosing projects for implementation is to select those with an economic rate of return higher than the opportunity cost of capital. Where resources are limited, projects are first ranked according to the economic rate of return. But that is not an end in itself. Projects are never selected on the basis of the economic rate of return alone. For one thing, the rate of return (like other measures of

---

6. Walter Schaefer-Kehnert, "How to Start an Internal Rate of Return Calculation," EDI Course Material, CN–30 (Washington, D.C.: World Bank, 1978; processed).

Table 4-4. *Calculation of Benefit/Cost Ratio and Net Present Worth: Method III. Positive Net Benefits Compared with Negative Net Benefits*
(thousands of Jamaican dollars)

Year	Investment costs (I)	Operation and maintenance costs (O+M)	Production costs (P)	Gross cost (I)+(O+M)+(P)	Gross benefits (B)	Net benefits	Discount factor at 12 percent	Present worth of net benefits at 12 percent
1	1,324	—	208	1,532	765	−767	0.893	−685
2	1,650	—	208	1,858	765	−1,093	0.797	−871
3	1,348	141	251	1,740	820	−920	0.712	−655
4	—	239	440	679	1,785	1,106	0.636	703
5	—	239	444	683	1,973	1,290	0.567	731
6	—	239	444	683	1,912	1,229	0.507	623
7	—	208	910	1,118	2,070	952	0.452	430
8–15	—	208[a]	915[a]	1,123[a]	2,127[a]	1,004[a]	2.247[d]	2,256
16	200	208	915	1,323	2,127	804	0.163	131
17–26	—	208[b]	915[b]	1,123[b]	2,127[b]	1,004[b]	0.922[e]	926
27	200	208	915	1,323	2,127	804	0.047	38
28–38	—	208[c]	915[c]	1,123[c]	2,127[c]	1,004[c]	0.278[f]	279
Total	4,722	7,514	31,270	43,506	76,027	32,521	8.221	3,906

Benefit/cost ratio at 12 percent = 6,117/2,211 = 2.77
Net present worth at 12 percent = J$6,117,000 − J$2,211,000 = J$3,906,000

— Not applicable.
a. Annual amount is included eight times in the total.
b. Annual amount is included ten times in the total.
c. Annual amount is included eleven times in the total.
Source: Same as for Table 4–2.

d. The present worth of an annuity factor for years 8 to 15.
e. The present worth of annuity factor for years 17 to 26.
f. The present worth of an annuity factor for years 28 to 38.

Table 4–5. *Calculation of Net Present Worth and Internal Rate of Return*
(thousands of Jamaican dollars)

Year	Gross costs	Gross benefits	Net benefits	Discount factor at 26 percent	Present worth at 26 percent	Discount factor at 31 percent	Present worth at 31 percent	Discount factor at 30 percent	Present worth at 30 percent
1	1,532	765	−767	0.794	−609	0.763	−585	0.769	−590
2	1,858	765	−1,093	0.630	−689	0.583	−637	0.592	−647
3	1,740	820	−920	0.500	−460	0.445	−409	0.455	−419
4	679	1,785	1,106	0.397	439	0.340	376	0.350	387
5	683	1,973	1,290	0.315	406	0.259	334	0.269	347
6	683	1,912	1,229	0.250	307	0.198	243	0.207	254
7	1,118	2,070	952	0.198	184	0.151	144	0.159	151
8–15	1,123[a]	2,127[a]	1,004[a]	0.643[d]	646	0.431[d]	433	0.466[d]	468
16	1,323	2,127	804	0.025	20	0.013	10	0.015	12
17–26	1,123[b]	2,127[b]	1,004[b]	0.086[e]	86	0.040[e]	40	0.047[e]	47
27	1,323	2,127	804	0.002	2	0.001	1	0.001	1
28–38	1,123[c]	2,127[c]	1,004[c]	0.007[f]	7	0.002[f]	2	0.002[f]	2
Total	43,506	76,027	32,521	3.847	339	3.226	−48	3.332	13

Internal rate of return = 26 + 5 [(339)/(387)] = 30 percent
Net present worth at 26 percent = J$339,000
Net present worth at 31 percent = J$48,000
Net present worth at 30 percent = J$13,000
Benefit/cost ratio at 30 percent = 1,669/1,656 = 1

a. Annual amount is included eight times in the total.
b. Annual amount is included ten times in the total.
c. Annual amount is included eleven times in the total.
Source: Same as for Table 4–2.

d. The present worth of an annuity factor for years 8 to 15.
e. The present worth of annuity factor for years 17 to 26.
f. The present worth of an annuity factor for years 28 to 38.

Table 4–6. *Financial Analysis for the Farm Family: Broiler Production Model*
(thousands of Philippine pesos)

		With project		
Item	Without project	Year 1	Years 2–7[a]	Years 8–10[a]
(a) Inflows				
Gross value of production	167.81	302.05	335.61	335.61
Loan receipts (90 percent of investment)	—	73.46	—	—
Total	167.81	375.51	335.61	335.61
(b) Outflows				
Investment costs	—	81.62	—	—
Cash operating expenses	143.46	232.41	288.14	288.14
Debt service	—	4.41	17.87	—
Total	143.46	318.44	306.01	288.14
(c) Farm family net benefit (a − b)	24.35	57.07	29.60	47.47
(d) Farm family net benefit without project[b]	24.35	24.35	24.35	24.35
(e) Incremental farm family net benefit (c − d)	—	32.72	5.25	23.12

Internal financial rate of return for the farm family = > 50 percent

— Not applicable.
a. Data in these columns are for each year of the period.
b. From the first column for item (c).
Source: Adapted from World Bank, "Appraisal of the Second Livestock Project-Philippines," 1070-PH (Washington, D.C., 1976, processed).

project worth) may not be precise because of faulty estimates or because of the impossibility of quantifying or valuing items of cost and benefit. Also the rate of return is only one criterion. Other important considerations include income distribution, creation of employment, transmission of technology, institution building, regional development, environmental protection, and defense. Social and political considerations sometimes exert a more powerful influence than the economic.

There is no single format for presenting the calculations of the financial and economic rates of return, but there are obvious advantages in adopting a system that sets out clearly the bases for the calculation. Table 4–6 presents a sample of one system. This format is modified for the calculation of the economic rate of return.

Net Benefit with and without the Project

The focus of agricultural project analysis is on the project's incremental net benefit stream. As shown in Table 4–6 the incremental net benefit is obtained by subtracting the net benefit without the project from the net benefit with the project. The net benefit without the project represents what the farm family would earn if the project were not implemented. It is equivalent to the opportunity cost for the labor, management, and existing capital (including land) contributed by the farm family. The incremental farm family net benefit, which is the surplus accruing from the project, is composed of two elements: (a) the return of capital to recover the investment made in the project, and (b) the return to capital to compensate for the use of the farm family resources invested in the project.

One of the most important principles in project analysis is to compare the situation with the project against the situation without the project. The situation before the project is not compared with that after the project. "Before the project" suggests an historical point in the past before the implementation of the project; it does not allow for assumptions about the future in the absence of the project. For some projects in areas where the level of productivity has been high, productivity could be expected to be stable, and the net benefit without the project to be as constant as in past years. The example in Table 4–6 shows a constant net benefit for the farm family (24,350 pesos) without the project. In such cases, it might be argued that it makes little difference whether the term "before the project" is used instead of "without the project." But this approach overlooks an important principle.

Situations do arise where the net benefit without the project does not remain constant. Even if the project were not implemented, productivity could increase because of earlier innovations or other investment activity. To say "before the project" and to assume that the net benefit would remain constant would be to overestimate the value of the project. Conversely, in analyzing a project where the area is suffering from impeded drainage, productivity would probably decrease if the project were not implemented. To assume that the net benefit would remain constant without the project would understate the value of the project. This situation is illustrated in Figure 4–1, which shows the projected gross values of production with and without the Upper Egypt drainage project. The justification for the project should not be based merely on the area between the with-project curve and the value of crop production at the inception

Figure 4–1.   *Upper Egypt Drainage Project:*
Projected Annual Value of Crop Production in the Project Area
Using Average Farm Gate Prices from 1967 to 1971

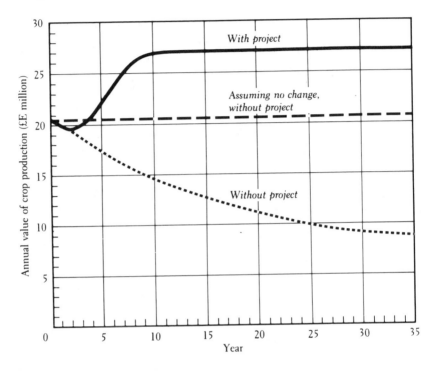

Source: World Bank, "Appraisal of Upper Egypt Drainage Project," 8-a-UAR (a restricted-circulation document) (Washington, D.C., 1973; processed).

of the project (£E20.5 million), but on the total area between the with-project curve and the without-project curve for the life of the project.

When it is expected that the farm family net benefit without the project would not remain constant, a separate table should be prepared to show the projection of the inflows, outflows, and the farm family net benefit without the project for the period corresponding to the life of the project.

Project Life

The life of a project is usually related to the productive life of the major assets. For example, the broiler production model in Table 4–6 has a project life of ten years, which is the estimated productive life of the poultry houses. Generally, agricultural project analysis rarely covers more than thirty-five years, although the productive life of the assets might last longer than fifty years. For example, Figure 4–1 assumes that the life of the Upper Egypt drainage project is thirty-five years. This does not necessarily mean that the irrigation system would become obsolete thirty-five years later. The limit was set at thirty-five years only because the discount factor would become so small by then that the present worth of the incremental net benefit stream would be too insignificant to have any effect on the internal rate of return.

5

•-•--•-•

Budgets for Land, Labor, and Capital in Agricultural Project Analysis

Complete budgeting or agricultural project analysis involves many stages. One of the first steps is to define the objectives, but not just in such broad terms as increased food production, introduction of soil conservation measures, provision of irrigation and drainage facilities, crop diversification, or import substitution. They should be translated into quantitative targets, for example, to produce a certain quantity or value of the commodities, to develop certain acreage, or to settle a certain number of farmers each year. Quantification of the objectives is crucial for the preparation, implementation, and evaluation of a project. It is equally important to prepare an inventory of available resources, taking into consideration the physical constraints and institutional restrictions that will be imposed on the project. Budgets should be prepared for each resource to coordinate demand and supply, to plan for efficient use, and to test the feasibility of the project. Resources may be conveniently divided into three broad categories: land, labor, and capital.

Land

Land serves two basic functions. It provides the space for production to take place, and it is the repository of the physical, chemical, and biological properties of nature. The different aspects of land to be considered for a project should include the location, soil, climate, vegetation, topography, and supply of terrestrial water.

Location determines the soil and climate of the project area. It also has a decisive effect on the accessibility of the project area, the communication facilities, the marketing opportunities, the supply of labor and other inputs, and the general attractiveness of the project to the participating farmers. The location of a project, particularly the relative advantages and disadvantages of the site, should be carefully described.

The soil and the climate are the two most important factors that determine the limits of crop and livestock production. The description of the soil should include details regarding classification, structure, texture, topography, pH, fertility, profile, deficiencies, degree of erosion, drainage, and depth of water table. Recommendations on soil management should also be made. Climate is defined as "the average course or conditions of the weather at a particular place over a period of many years as exhibited by the absolute extremes, means, and frequencies of given departures from the means, of temperature, wind velocity, precipitation, and other weather elements."[1] Description of the climate should cover the elements mentioned in this definition, as well as seasonal information relating to hours of sunlight, length of the growing season, and the history of floods, drought, or other natural phenomena that could seriously affect production.

The inventory of land resources should also show the total area of the project, the arable acreage, the types of land use patterns and farming methods, the physical yields for each crop and livestock enterprise under different seasonal conditions and levels of management, and the influence of institutional factors (such as land tenure arrangements and inheritance laws) on farm fragmentation and levels of productivity. The more comprehensive an inventory, the easier it is to prepare the budget for land.

A budget for land resources is necessary to select cropping sequences and combinations that will yield the optimum level of income in a particular environment and within the scope of a particular project. If the project is designed to produce a single crop, the inventory of land resources will indicate whether the conditions of the project area are favorable for producing that crop. Quite often the overall objective of a project is to produce a wide range of crops. Then a decision has to be made on the kinds of crops to grow, the acreage to be allocated to each crop, and the cropping sequence. Final answers cannot be provided until the budgets for all factors of production are prepared and until the costs and returns for alternative production systems are analyzed. Preliminary answers may be obtained by considering alternative rotational programs.

1. *Webster's Third International Dictionary*, Philip Babcock (ed.), 7th ed. (Springfield, Mass.: G. and C. Merriam, 1966).

Rotational cropping usually has significant advantages over monocropping. Crops grown in combination or in a particular sequence often have a beneficial effect on one another. An effective crop rotational program would prevent soil erosion, maintain soil productivity, help soil drainage, and control weeds, diseases, and pests. It will allow for soil-building crops frequently on each field and will select the crops most adapted to each type of soil. It will spread labor, machinery, and power over the season, and will adjust to rainfall limitations and moisture needs. It will also lessen risks and uncertainties, provide livestock feed and cash income, and use the land for the most profitable crops.[2]

A rotational program provides a useful framework for long-term planning, but it should not be an inflexible constraint. Like any other plan, it merely provides the blueprint for systematic management. Unexpected climatic conditions may occur in particular seasons, or the demand and supply for particular crops may change, making it necessary to modify the rotational program from time to time.

Valuing land in financial analysis

Land is valued differently in financial analysis and in economic analysis. But in both cases the calculation is based on the form of tenure and whether or not transfer of ownership is involved.

If a tenant farmer rents land to participate in a project, the annual rent he pays will be shown in the financial analysis as an outflow each year during the life of the project. If the farmer has rented and used the land before the project has begun, the annual rent would be reflected in the outflow streams with and without the project. If the land is made available to the farmer free of charge, no cost would be shown.

Where the farmer purchases the land to participate in a project, a transfer of ownership is involved. If the full price is paid in one installment, the actual amount paid will be shown as an outflow in the year in which payment is to be made. If the price is paid by installments, the annual payments will be reflected as outflows as they are made.

Where the land was previously owned by the farmer, there would be no transfer of ownership, nor any payment to purchase or rent the land for the project. But an estimate would have to be made of the opportunity cost or the income the family gives up by using the land differently from the past. If the farmer were not earning an income from the land, there would be no income foregone. If the farmer had rented the land to someone

---

2. Earl O. Heady and Harold R. Jensen, *Farm Management Economics* (Englewood Cliffs: Prentice-Hall, 1954), p. 122.

else, the annual rent he used to receive would be the income foregone. If the farmer used the land himself, he would be the owner-operator, and the valuation of the land would be the annual income the farmer normally expected to receive from it without the project. In Table 4–6, Chapter 4, the farm family net benefit without the project represents the opportunity cost: the income the farm family gives up by transferring the use of the land to the project. It is the return for the farm family's land, labor, management, and existing capital. In subtracting the farm family net benefit without the project from the farm family net benefit in each year of the project life, the opportunity cost of the farm family's land, labor, management, and existing capital is at the same time taken into account.

An interesting case for analysis is the sharecropping arrangement, in which the landlord and tenant use the land jointly and share both expenses and the resulting crop. Usually the landlord provides the land, management, and other inputs, whereas the sharecropper supplies labor and pays for some operating expenses. Production is proportionally shared between the landlord and the sharecropper according to the terms of the arrangement.

Financial analysis can be prepared for either the sharecropper or the landlord or both, since they share in the income and expenses of the farm. If it is for the sharecropper, the land can be valued in two different ways. In the first method, the tenant's share of the expenses would be shown as outflows and his share of production as inflows. In the second method, the total value of production from the farm could be entered as inflows, but the landlord's share of production would be an outflow in lieu of rent. If the analysis is for the landlord, the land would be valued in a way similar to that for an owner-operator, but only the landlord's share of expenses would be outflows and his share of the income would be inflows. If the total value of production were shown as an inflow, the tenant's share of production would have to be shown as an outflow.

Valuing land in economic analysis

In preparing the economic analysis, land is valued at its true economic cost or at the net value of production foregone. This net value would be the market price if there were a perfect market for land. As Gittinger puts it, "In this perfect market we would be indifferent if we chose to value land at its purchase price, at its rental value or at the value of its net contribution to production; each would be equivalent to the other."[3] The

---

3. J. Price Gittinger, *Economic Analysis of Agricultural Projects* (Baltimore: Johns Hopkins University Press, 1972), p. 16.

market for land, however, is far from perfect. Speculative expectations or other considerations, such as social prestige and personal security, sometimes have stronger influence on the market price than the land's net contribution to production.

Where the project does not involve a change in land ownership, the economic value of the land is the net value of production foregone. This value would be calculated in the same way as in a financial analysis, but the items of cost and benefit would be valued at shadow prices, which are discussed in Chapter 8. Where a change in land ownership is involved, the purchase price might overstate the true economic cost. It might then be necessary to estimate the annual income-earning capacity of the land. In the absence of precise data, the annual rent for similar land may be taken as a reasonable estimate. If the land was lying idle, the true economic cost would be zero. If the land was used for some purpose, such as for pasture or recreation facilities, asssessment of the benefit from such use would be the basis for estimating the income foregone or its opportunity cost.

Valuing land—a summary

The rules for estimating the value of land in agricultural project analysis are summarized below. In financial analysis, costs and benefits are measured at market prices; in economic analysis, at shadow prices.

Condition	Financial analysis (based on market prices)	Economic analysis (based on shadow prices)
(a) Owner-operator on land purchased with the project.	Use purchase price.	Use annual income-earning capacity or annual rent for similar land. (If the land was idle, the rent would be zero.)
(b) Owner-operator on land owned with and without the project.	Value of land included in farm family net benefit without the project.	Value of land included in net benefit without the project. (If the land was idle, the value would be zero.)
(c) Tenant renting land with the project.	Use rent paid.	As in (a), above.
(d) Tenant renting land with and without the project.	As in (c), above.	As in (b), above.
(e) Tenant operating land free of cost with the project.	No cost.	As in (a), above.

Condition	Financial analysis (based on market prices)	Economic analysis (based on shadow prices)
(f) Tenant operating land free of cost with and without the project.	No cost.	As in (b), above.
(g) Land purchased with the project and operated under a sharecropping arrangement.	For landlord, use purchase price; for sharecropper, show rent as zero and sharecropper's portion of income as an inflow. or Show landlord's share of income as a cost and total production as inflow.	As in (a), above.
(h) Land operated under a sharecropping arrangement with and without the project.	For landlord, as in (b), above; for sharecropper, as in (g) above.	As in (b), above.

Residual value of land

Calculating the residual or salvage value of land at the end of the project raises some interesting issues. Unlike other assets, which depreciate in value over time, land may appreciate in value. This increase in value should be reflected in both financial and economic analysis. It is important, however, to differentiate between the increase which would accrue even without the project and that which would accrue solely because of the project. To reflect an increase in the residual value of land that could accrue even without the project would overstate the project's benefits. To correct this, it is necessary to estimate the residual values with and without the project, calculate the net residual value, and then enter it as an inflow in the final year of the project. But the estimate of the internal economic or financial rate of return is generally not affected by the residual value of land or of any other asset, except in cases where the life of the project is very short, where the residual value of assets is very large relative to the net benefit stream, or where the internal rate of return is very low.

Labor

Labor is the most substantial input contributed by the farm family in most agricultural projects. Land is usually made available to farmers on a freehold or leasehold basis by the government or project authority. Most of the capital is often provided through grants, loans, and subsidies; the farmer's contribution from his own resources rarely exceeds 20 percent of the investment. But the farm family invariably supplies most of the labor on small farms. In many agricultural projects in developing countries, the size of the farm is often directly related to the acreage the family can manage.

Since labor constitutes such an important part of the family's contribution, it should be examined carefully in planning agricultural projects. Some of the necessary information can be obtained from census reports and sample survey data provided by government statistical agencies. It is often necessary, however, to carry out additional surveys to obtain specific information about family labor and the probable sources of hired labor. In estimating the supply of family labor, the analyst needs detailed information about the members of the household, such as their age, sex, educational background, professional experience, preferences for crop and livestock, and the number of hours they are likely to work on the farm in different periods of the year. In estimating the probable sources of hired labor, the analyst needs information on the surrounding area as to the usual sources of employment, the seasonal pattern of unemployment, transport facilities, and wage rates. The more data the analyst has on the quantity and distribution of family and hired labor, the easier it will be for him to prepare budgets to test the technical and economic feasibility of alternative farming programs.

Measuring labor productivity

To prepare these budgets, the supply of labor must be aggregated. This would be relatively simple if labor were homogeneous. But the quality of labor varies according to the worker's age, sex, health, nutrition, and experience; the level of technology; and the nature of the work. Many analysts use a common measure, the man-day, which is based on the amount of productive work that the average adult male worker can perform within an eight to ten hour day. Some analysts have also derived conversion factors to express labor performed by women and children in terms of man-days. These conversion factors are usually based on comparative wage rates and assumptions about the productivities of different types of labor. For example, Yang's system[4] converts woman-days and child-days into man-days by assigning a ratio of: 2 child-days = 1.25 woman-days = 1 man-equivalent day. But these attempts at standardization have not been

4. W. Y. Yang, *Methods of Farm Management Investigations* (Rome: Food and Agricultural Organization, 1965), p. 61.

universally accepted. In his study of small-scale farming in Jamaica, Edwards decides not to use conversion factors to adjust labor; his reasoning is:

> If conversion factors were to have been helpful rather than misleading they would have to take account of more than age and sex characteristics of the workers because capacity of work differs even between two persons of the same age and sex. But adjusting the labor used on each farm on its own merits would have involved making numerous value judgments of doubtful validity. For these reasons it seemed preferable to add together the actual hours of work undertaken by different people. This measure has the virtue that its limitations are obvious.[5]

In his study on Zaïre,[6] Tollens contends that "in the final analysis, any conversion of female and child labor to man labor units is arbitrary." He believed that women in Zaïre were as efficient as men in the types of work performed. Therefore in his analysis he adopted the scale proposed by Spencer,[7] whereby children from seven to fifteen were assigned a weight of 0.5 and women a weight of 1.0.

Experience throughout the world has shown that it is a fallacy to assume that a woman's effective output is always less than a man's. Besides, work assignments on the farm are highly specialized. Some jobs are assigned to women not merely because they are "a woman's work" in the derogatory sense, but because a woman's productive capacity at such jobs has proved to be greater than a man's. An interesting photograph is presented in Kyeyune Ssentongo's study on the farming system in the high altitude areas of the Ankole district in Uganda.[8] The picture shows the outcome of a contest between a farmer's wife and a male extension worker in harvesting finger millet. The male extension worker lost the contest both in terms of the quantity harvested and the quality of the product. Ssentongo's comment is: "you just cannot beat a professional." His study also

5. David Edwards, *Economic Study of Small Farming in Jamaica* (Kingston University of the West Indies, Institute of Social and Economic Research, 1961), p. 345.

6. Eric F. Tollens, "Problems of Micro-Economic Data Collection on Farms in Northern Zaire," Working Paper, no. 7 (East Lansing, Michigan: Department of Agricultural Economics, Michigan State University, June 1975; processed), p. 18.

7. Dunstan S. C. Spencer, "Micro-Level Farm Management and Production Economics Research Among Traditional African Farmers: Lessons from Sierra Leone," African Rural Employment Paper, no. 3 (East Lansing, Michigan: Department of Agricultural Economics, Michigan State University, 1972; processed).

8. Kyeyune Ssentongo, "An Economic Survey of the High Altitude Areas of Ankole" (Uganda Ministry of Agriculture, Forestry and Cooperatives, 1973; processed), p. 24.

shows that it usually takes 179 hours to weed an acre of finger millet. Of this work, the farmer puts in only 7 percent; the wife, 75. The rest is contributed by children and hired labor.

On balance, therefore, there is little justification for distinguishing between male and female adult labor on the farm. Significant differences, of course, would justify making a distinction, as in the case of child labor. But it is both convenient and reasonable to aggregate male and female adult labor in the same way, without applying a conversion factor to the latter.

Labor budgets

The supply of adult labor is relatively evenly distributed throughout the year. The demand for labor varies, however, with different enterprises and fluctuates widely with the season, being heaviest in the planting and harvesting periods.

The farmer will try, if possible, to select a variety of enterprises as a hedge against uncertainty. He will try to distribute evenly the demand for labor, provide a steady flow of income, or secure a beneficial rotational program. He will arrange the enterprises either in combination or in sequence; in either case there is the risk of bottlenecks from overlapping or improper phasing. Labor budgets provide a solution to this problem. The budgets, which are based on the labor requirements of each crop, compare the aggregate demand for and supply of labor on the farm.

Labor as a resource is the amount of work performed by people, not just the people themselves.[9] It should be considered as a flow resource rather than a stock. Unlike capital, it cannot be stored. Labor that is not used one day is not available on the next. Therefore labor budgets should ideally be prepared at least on a daily basis. This is how the farmer operates, but it would be impractical for project analysts. As a compromise, labor budgets are usually prepared on a monthly or seasonal basis. Comparison of the aggregate monthly supply of and requirements for labor on the farm will reveal the periods of deficits and surpluses. Supplementary enterprises can be introduced to utilize surplus labor as long as their gross margins are positive and their management is technically feasible.

If the family cannot supply all the labor needed for the enterprises, there are several optional remedies: modify the size of some enterprises, vary the cropping sequence, or hire labor on a casual or full-time basis depending on the length of the period or on the nature of the deficit. In

9. Martin Upton, *Farm Management in Africa* (London: Oxford University Press, 1973), p. 126.

many countries informal arrangements are adopted to help farmers over-
come seasonal deficits or to tackle particular jobs that need to be done
expeditiously. These arrangements include the right to use land, buildings,
machinery, or animals in lieu of wages; "morning sport," where farmers
in turn provide a feast and entertainment at the end of a task on the farm
as compensation for communal labor; and "day for day," where the farmer
is obliged to supply his own labor in exchange for similar help obtained
from other farmers.

The information on the labor required for the enterprises is derived from
labor profiles prepared for each enterprise on the farm. For convenience
and easier aggregation, these profiles are based on units of land measurement, such as one acre, one feddan, or one hectare.[10] They show the
number of man-days required for each operation in each month for the
duration of each crop. The data are usually derived from observations by
extension officers, research experience, farm records, and informal surveys.
Labor requirements for similar operations on different farms usually vary
because of the worker's age, sex, health, nutrition, and motivation, or
because of soil conditions. Significant differences also occur under different
levels of mechanization, and therefore it is customary to prepare separate
profiles for each level. Where the farm uses farm machinery pools or has
certain tasks performed on contract, these operations should be shown
separately in the labor profile, since they do not make use of the labor
generally available on the farm.

Labor force surveys provide data relating to family composition and the
contribution of each family member to productive labor. In the context
of agricultural project analysis, productive labor refers to the number of
hours each family member is able and willing to work on an income-
earning activity included in the project. Thus, it normally excludes time
for leisure, employment outside the farm, and any other activity that does
not directly contribute to the output of the project. In estimating family
labor, allowance must be made for illness in the family, school attendance,
housework, leisure, domestic and social commitments, employment outside the farm, and other pursuits that are not related directly to activities
on the farm which earn income. Separate budgets should be prepared to
reflect demand and supply without the project and at different stages during
the life of the project, so that it may be determined whether the farm
family can cope with the revised farm program and what outside labor
might be required.

Tables 5–1 to 5–6 illustrate the preparation of labor profiles, using data

10. 1 feddan = 1.038 acres; 1 hectare = 2.47 acres.

derived from studies on the cost of production conducted in Jamaica. These profiles will then be aggregated to prepare the labor budget in Table 5–7. It is assumed that two rotational programs are practiced on the four-acre farm, each rotation covering three crops in the year, as shown below:

Rotation A: two acres	Rotation B: two acres
Irish potato (January to April)	Carrot (January to April)
Watermelon (May to August)	Peanut (May to July)
Lettuce (September to December)	Tomato (August to December)

Each crop program may finish a few days before or after the end of a calendar month, or may start shortly before or after the beginning of a calendar month. But for the sake of convenience, it is assumed that its beginning and end coincide with calendar months.

In this illustration, labor is supplied by contract (custom work), by hired temporary labor, and by the farmer and his wife. The farmer works twenty-five days a month. The wife contributes up to thirteen days a month. Hired temporary labor supplies the balance.

Labor profiles for each of the six crops in the rotational program show the operations, the source of labor, and the number of man-days required each month for one acre of the crop. Since two crops are produced each month, each crop on two acres, the total labor required for the four-acre farm is obtained by first adding the requirement for each acre of the crops and then by doubling the sum, as shown in the labor budget in Table 5–7.

Table 5–1. *Labor Profile for Irish Potato, Rotation A*

Operations	Source of labor	Labor requirement (man-days)				
		January	February	March	April	Total
Land clearing	Contract	6	...	...	...	6
Ploughing	Contract	15	...	...	...	15
Refining	Contract	12	...	...	...	12
Furrowing	Contract	10	...	...	...	10
Planting and fertilizing	Farm	10	...	...	...	10
Weeding and moulding	Farm	...	4	...	...	4
Spraying	Farm	...	2	4	...	6
Reaping	Farm	...	...	...	10	10
Total		53	6	4	10	73

Note: Area = 1 acre; duration of crop = 4 months.
... Zero or negligible.
Source: Adapted from data prepared by the Agricultural Planning Unit, Ministry of Agriculture, Jamaica.

Hired labor is supplied to make up the difference between the demand and the total supply from custom work, the farmer, and his wife.

The labor budget shows that the farm depends heavily on outside labor during May and between August and January. If outside labor were not available, the farm program would have to be modified substantially.

Table 5–2. *Labor Profile for Watermelon, Rotation A*

Operation	Source of labor	Labor requirement (man-days)				
		May	June	July	August	Total
Land clearing	Contract	7	...	...	...	7
Digging holes and moulding	Farm	10	...	...	...	10
Fertilizing	Farm	1	...	...	...	1
Staking (to mark holes)	Farm	6	...	...	...	6
Planting	Farm	8	...	...	...	8
Weeding	Farm	...	10	...	...	10
Spraying	Farm	...	1	1	...	2
Reaping	Farm	...	...	...	8	8
Total		32	11	1	8	52

Note: Area = 1 acre; duration of crop = 4 months.
... Zero or negligible.
Source: Same as for Table 5–1.

Table 5–3. *Labor Profile for Lettuce, Rotation A*

Operation	Source of labor	Labor requirement (man-days)				
		September	October	November	December	Total
Ploughing	Contract	15	...	...	...	15
Refining	Contract	15	...	...	...	15
Planting	Farm	10	...	...	...	10
Fertilizing	Farm	1	...	...	...	1
Weeding and moulding	Farm	...	10	10	...	20
Spraying	Farm	...	1	1	...	2
Reaping	Farm	...	...	...	15	15
Total		41	11	11	15	78

Note: Area = 1 acre; duration of crop = 4 months.
... Zero or negligible.
Source: Same as for Table 5–1.

Valuing labor

In valuing labor for project analysis, it is important to distinguish between family labor and hired labor. The family is not normally paid a wage, and family labor is not treated as an item of cost in farm accounting. Hired labor (whether in the form of custom, job, or piece work; or full-time, part-time, permanent, or temporary employment), however, is included in the cost. In financial or economic analysis, this method is

Table 5–4. *Labor Profile for Carrot, Rotation B*

| Operation | Source of labor | Labor requirement (man-days) | | | | |
		January	February	March	April	Total
Land clearing	Contract	6	...	...	...	6
Ploughing	Contract	15	...	...	...	15
Refining	Contract	12	...	...	...	12
Planting	Farm	10	...	...	...	10
Fertilizing	Farm	1	...	...	...	1
Weeding	Farm	5	15	10	...	30
Reaping	Farm	...	...	...	6	6
Total		49	15	10	6	80

Note: Area = 1 acre; duration of crop = 4 months.
... Zero or negligible.
Source: Same as for Table 5–1.

Table 5–5. *Labor Profile for Peanuts, Rotation B*

| Operation | Source of labor | Labor requirement (man-days) | | | |
		May	June	July	Total
Ploughing and harrowing	Contract	15	...	...	15
Furrowing	Contract	10	...	...	10
Planting and fertilizing	Farm	5	...	...	5
Weeding and moulding	Farm	4	6	...	10
Spraying	Farm	...	2	1	3
Harvesting	Farm	...	...	12	12
Total		34	8	13	55

Note: Area = 1 acre; duration of crop = 3 months.
... Zero or negligible.
Source: Same as for Table 5–1.

maintained, but with one important modification: the principle of opportunity cost is applied to reflect the value of family labor.

FAMILY LABOR. The opportunity cost of family labor is the income from the next best alternative that is foregone by participating in the project. Generally it is incorporated in the farm family net benefit without the project if the family operates the farm full-time without the project. If participation in the project necessitates an increase in family labor on the farm so that income earned outside the farm was either reduced or eliminated, however, any income sacrificed should be added to the farm family net benefit without the project to reflect the full opportunity cost of family labor. The same principle would apply in valuing labor from a family that was not previously engaged in farming. Market prices are used to estimate the income foregone in financial analysis; shadow prices are used in economic analysis.

It has been mentioned before that the farm family net benefit without the project represents the family's reward for investing their land, labor, management, and capital in activities they would engage in without the project. Therefore when the farm family net benefit without the project is subtracted from the net benefit stream flowing from the project, the opportunity cost of family labor is automatically taken into consideration. The resulting incremental farm family net benefit stream represents the

Table 5–6. *Labor Profile for Tomato, Rotation B*

Operation	Source of labor	August	September	October	November	December	Total
						Labor requirement (man-days)	
Ploughing	Contract	15	...	...	...	...	15
Digging holes	Farm	5	...	...	...	...	5
Fertilizing	Farm	6	...	...	...	...	6
Planting	Farm	6	...	...	...	...	6
Weeding and moulding	Farm	...	10	...	...	...	10
Staking	Farm	...	4	...	...	...	4
Pruning	Farm	...	10	10	...	...	20
Spraying	Farm	...	4	3	...	...	7
Reaping	Farm	...	...	...	20	10	30
Grading and packing	Farm	...	...	...	10	5	15
Total		32	28	13	30	15	118

Note: Area = 1 acre; duration of crop = 5 months.
... Zero or negligible.
Source: Same as for Table 5–1.

Table 5-7. Labor Budget for the Farm
(man-days a month)

Labor demand and supply	January	February	March	April	May	June	July	August	September	October	November	December	Total
Labor demand—1 acre													
Irish potato, Rotation A	53	6	4	10	...	...	...	...	...	...	...	...	73
Watermelon, Rotation A	...	...	...	...	32	11	1	8	...	...	...	...	52
Lettuce, Rotation A	...	...	...	...	...	...	...	...	41	11	11	15	78
Carrot, Rotation B	49	15	10	6	...	...	...	...	...	...	...	...	80
Peanut, Rotation B	...	...	...	...	34	8	13	...	...	...	...	...	55
Tomato, Rotation B	...	...	...	...	...	...	...	32	28	13	30	15	118
Total demand—two acres	102	21	14	16	66	19	14	40	69	24	41	30	456
Total demand—four acres	204	42	28	32	132	38	28	80	138	48	82	60	912
Labor supply													
Custom work (contract)	152	...	...	...	64	...	...	30	60	...	...	...	306
Farmer	25	25	25	25	25	25	25	25	25	25	25	25	300
Wife	13	13	3	7	13	13	3	13	13	13	13	13	130
Hired labor	14	4	...	...	30	...	...	12	40	10	44	22	176
Total supply—four acres	204	42	28	32	132	38	28	80	138	48	82	60	912

... Zero or negligible.
Source: Same as for Table 5-1.

return for only the capital invested in the project but not for farm family labor, management, or land.

HIRED LABOR. In preparing a financial analysis, hired labor is simply valued in terms of the market wage rate. In an economic analysis, however, it is valued at its opportunity cost, also called the shadow wage. This opportunity cost reflects the contribution that the labor employed in the project could make to economic growth elsewhere in society. Market wages often differ from the opportunity cost because of minimum wage laws, union representation, social conventions, employer's attitudes, and other elements of imperfect competition in society. These influences may not be strong in the market for agricultural labor, but when there is a high level of unemployment in the society, a new project can absorb labor without reducing the level of production elsewhere in the society. Thus, many economists argue that the opportunity cost of labor is perhaps as low as zero in developing countries.[11] In valuing labor for an economic analysis, skilled labor must be distinguished from the unskilled, unemployed labor from the underemployed and the fully employed, and slack season labor from the peak season.

Valuation of skilled labor in developing countries for the economic analysis presents little problem. Skilled labor is almost always in short supply, so that the market wage rate is generally a good reflection of its true opportunity cost. Unskilled labor presents considerable difficulty, however, and each situation must be judged on its own merits. The only possible generalization is that the opportunity cost of unskilled labor is likely to be somewhat less than its market price, but it is debatable whether it is as low as zero, as some analysts contend. If unskilled labor is fully employed without the project, it is valued at the market wage rate; if it is underemployed without the project, it is valued at the wage rate for the peak season multiplied by the numbers of days when labor is critical; if it is unemployed without the project, it is valued at the cost of bringing labor to the project. Such costs may include transport, housing, or other incentives that might have to be provided, and should be included among project costs in the economic analysis. If the labor would be unemployed without the project, the shadow wage rate usually would be close to zero.

11. See Stephen J. Ettinger, "Nigeria: The Opportunity Cost of Rural Labor," research paper prepared for the World Bank (Washington, D.C., 1973; processed); also Charles H. C. Kao, Kurt R. Anschel, and Carl K. Eicher, "Disguised Unemployment in Agriculture: A Survey," in Carl Eicher and Lawrence Witt (ed.), *Agriculture in Economic Development*, (New York: McGraw-Hill, 1964), pp. 129–44.

Valuing labor—a summary

The rules for valuing labor in agricultural projects are summarized below:

Condition	Financial analysis *(based on market prices)*	Economic analysis *(based on shadow prices)*
Family labor		
Family on farm full-time without the project.	The opportunity cost of labor is incorporated in the farm family net benefit without the project, which is to be subtracted from the net benefit stream with the project.	Same principle as in financial analysis.
Family not on farm full-time without the project; increased family labor input required with the project.	Add off-farm income foregone to farm-family-net-benefit-without-the-project.	Same principle as in financial analysis.
Family not operating the farm without the project but engaged in other income-earning activities.	Deduct estimated income foregone from the farm family net benefit stream with the project.	Same principle as in financial analysis.
Hired labor		
Skilled labor.	Use market wage rate.	Use the market wage rate as the shadow price.
Unskilled labor		
Unemployed without the project.	Use market wage rate.	Shadow wage rate may be close to zero, but include costs necessary to attract labor to the area.
Fully employed without the project.	Use market wage rate.	Use the market wage rate as the shadow price.
Underemployed without the project.	Use market wage rate.	Use wage rate for peak seasons multiplied by the number of days when labor is scarce.

Capital

The word "capital" has numerous definitions, but in this study it is only necessary to distinguish between two concepts of capital: as a physical resource and as a financial resource.

Budgeting capital as a physical resource

As a physical resource capital comprises those goods that produce other goods. Capital goods include such items as plant, machinery, buildings, and breeding animals. They are distinguished from raw materials, such as fertilizer, seed, and chemicals, which are commonly called noncapital goods. Capital goods usually have a longer productive life than one production period. In the process of production the capital good is progressively worn out or depreciated. In conventional accounting, which shows the annual net profit of a firm, expenses include only the annualized value of depreciation, not the full cost of the capital good.

The distinction between capital and noncapital goods is maintained in agricultural project analysis. But all items, whether capital or noncapital, enter directly into the cost stream in the year when the expenditure is expected. It is not necessary, therefore, to include depreciation as an item of cost in either financial or economic analysis. To include it would be double counting.

The nature of the land, the composition of the labor force, the choice of enterprises, and the size of the operation will determine the types and quantities of required inputs. For proper planning, resource budgets should be prepared for each of the main enterprises, for representative farm units, and for the total project. They should be prepared on a monthly or at least quarterly basis to reflect the seasonal requirements of the farm.

Resource budgets expressed in physical quantities rather than value usually cover such items as transport, machinery, tools, equipment, fertilizers, chemicals, and other inputs procured from off-farm sources. But the success of many projects has been jeopardized because of the lack of planning for the supply of inputs produced on the farm, such as seedlings, suckers, cuttings, weaners, calves, in-calf heifers, and other intermediate goods. In some projects these items are produced in central nurseries or research stations, with the project authority being responsible for their procurement and distribution to the farmers. In other projects farmers are expected to make their own arrangement. In too many projects, however, there is no clear policy, so that neither the project authority nor the farmer is responsible for ensuring that inputs are available in the necessary quantities and at the proper time and place.

Comprehensive budgets should show the scheduling of the physical inputs required for the project, for each enterprise on the farm, and for the farm as a whole. They should indicate what items will be needed, when they will be needed, and how they will be supplied. Responsibility for the procurement of inputs should be clearly defined, and the farmers

Table 5-8. *Budget for Financial Resources for the Farm Only*

Item	January	February	March	April	May	June	July	August	September	October	November	December	Total
Cash inflows													
Produce sales receipts													
Livestock sales receipts													
Land sales/rent receipts													
Other sales receipts													
Grants, susidies, gifts in cash													
Loans													
Other cash inflows													
Total													
Cash outflows													
Cash farm operating expenditures													
Livestock purchase expenditures													
Machinery purchase expenditures													
Land purchase/rent expenditures													
Farm taxes paid													
Loan interest paid													
Loan repayments													
Other cash expenses													
Total													
Surplus													
Deficit													
Positive balance													
Negative balance													

and the project authority should coordinate constantly during the implementation of the project.

Budgeting capital as a financial resource

The monetary concept of capital relates to the flow of financial resources into the project. They enable the farmers who participate in the project to acquire goods and services required to produce the projected output. In common practice they are generally referred to as fixed or working capital, or as long-, medium- or short-term capital. They are usually derived from sales, loans, grants, gifts, subsidies, or equity participation.

In agricultural project analysis, three types of financial budgets are required: a budget to calculate the financial rate of return; a budget to calculate the economic rate of return; and a budget to test the liquidity of the project. The last is particularly important in the early life of the project. Some confusion arises because these budgets are sometimes called by a common name, cash flow. But the rules for treating financial resources in these three types of budgets are different.

The financial rate of return determines the return on the investment by each project entity. Thus, in calculating the rate of return on the farm family's investment, the farm family's contribution of capital is not included as an inflow. The excess of the outflows over the inflows reflects the farm family's contribution. All other financial resources outside the farm—such as grants, loans, and subsidies—are treated as inflows in the year they are expected.

The economic rate of return determines the return to the whole society on all resources committed to the project, regardless of equity participation. In economic analysis, it is assumed that all the resources used in the project belong to someone in the society. Thus, neither inflows of loans or grants nor outflows for debt servicing are reflected. This treatment will also apply for foreign loans that could be used for other projects in the country.[12]

The third type of financial budget, which reflects a project's liquidity, can be called the budget for financial resources. It shows only market transactions that affect the amount of cash a farm would have at its disposal in different periods. It translates the budget for labor and physical resources into financial terms and makes it easy to compare cash inflows and outflows in each period. For subsistence and semisubsistence farms where most of the output is consumed in the home, this type of budget is particularly useful. For example, in preparing the financial analysis to obtain the

12. Gittinger, *Economic Analysis of Agricultural Projects*, p. 69.

Table 5–9. Budget for Financial Resources for the Farm/Home Complex

Item	January	February	March	April	May	June	July	August	September	October	November	December	Total
Cash inflows													
Produce sales receipts													
Livestock sales receipts													
Land sales/rent receipts													
Other sales receipts													
Grants, susidies, gifts in cash													
Cash income earned outside farm													
Loans													
Other cash inflows													
Total													
Cash outflows													
Cash farm operating expenditures													
Livestock purchase expenditures													
Machinery purchase expenditures													
Land purchase/rent expenditures													
Farm taxes paid													
Loan interest paid													
Loan repayments													
Household expenses													
Family taxes paid													
Other cash expenses													
Total													
Surplus													
Deficit													
Positive balance													
Negative balance													

financial rate of return, the gross value of production is derived by multiplying total production by farm gate prices. But this value overstates the cash inflow, since total production includes portions that are consumed in the home. Similarly the rental value of the farm is included, but it is not a cash inflow. Thus, to show the actual cash position of the farm, it is necessary to prepare a separate financial budget.

Projections for cash and credit transactions are usually made annually. But annual projections invariably mask imbalances that occur during the year. This consideration is particularly important in planning agricultural projects that involve excessive expenditure at the beginning of the project. Ideally the budget for financial resources should show projections for the sources and uses of funds on a monthly basis at least for the first three years, depending on the nature of the project.

In cases where household expenses can be separated from farm operations, a budget should be prepared for the farm only. The items to be entered for each month of the year are listed below. This budget, which should reflect the cash and credit transactions relating only to the farm, will include in the inflows only that portion of output expected to be sold, revenue from other sales, and the farm family's investment, loans, grants, and subsidies to be received in cash, as shown in Table 5–8.

The interdependence between the farm as a business and the farm as a home is sometimes so strong on semisubsistence farms, however, that it is virtually impossible to separate the two functions. The financial resources of the family are often used to meet business expenses, and the financial resources of the business are often channeled into private household expenditures. Many development projects have been jeopardized because project planners and government administrators, failing to appreciate this fact, did not forestall the dissipation of farm development funds on household expenses. Where the farm and the home cannot be differentiated, a budget for the farm/home complex should be prepared. This budget should include income earned outside the farm and family living expenses, as shown in Table 5–9.

A surplus or a deficit represents the difference between cash outflows and inflows of each production period, which may be monthly, quarterly, annually, or any other period necessitated by the nature of the project. A positive or a negative balance reflects the cumulative cash position from the beginning of the project up to the end of each period. It incorporates surplus and deficits for all previous periods.

A negative balance would indicate that additional credit or financing is necessary to meet expenses up to the end of the period. It does not indicate that the farm is necessarily operating at a loss. To determine the profitability of the farm it is necessary to calculate the net farm income, as illustrated in Table 2–8.

6

●-●--●--●--●-●--●-●--●--●-●--●--●-●--●-●--●--●-●--●--●-●--●--●-●--●-●--●--●-●--●--●-●--●--●-●--●-●--●--●-●--●--●-●--●-●--●-●--●--●-●--●.

Farm Models

An agricultural development project is sometimes designed specifically to produce a certain amount of a particular crop or livestock. Quite often, however, projects have indirect objectives that involve land reclamation, soil conservation, irrigation, drainage, pasture development, or measures for increasing productivity, introducing new enterprises, or expanding crop or livestock production. These projects range from the simple to the complex, from the production of a single crop to that of different crops, of different livestock, or of crops and livestock combined.

A project is not always located in a single geographic zone having homogenous physical resources and economic and social infrastructure. Even within one geographic area, there may be considerable variation in soil types, size of farms, production systems, quality of management, or other important factors. If the project consists of a single farm, one set of budgets for the factors of production would be sufficient to plan the rotation system, to calculate farm income, and to project the value of inflows and outflows over the life of the project. But if the project consists of several farms, a single set of budgets may not be adequate to represent the characteristics of the different farms in the analysis of the project's technical feasibility and its profitability. When the farms are similar, one of them may be selected as a representative; but when the farms are different, they should be separated into relatively homogenous groups, within which only minor variations exist. These groups would form the bases for farm models.

A farm model is a simplified representation of a farm. It is used to typify the different kinds of farming situations that may be found in a project and serves two important functions: to facilitate analysis of the project's effect on the various groups of participating farmers, and to prepare for the aggregation of the project's total costs and benefits.

The number of models that should be prepared for each project depends on the characteristics of the particular project. It could be as large as the number of farms in a project, because no two farms are completely alike. But this would be impractical in a large project. If the project takes place on existing farms, the type of farming system, the size of the farm, and the level of management will help to determine the number of models. If the project is to develop a new area or to settle farmers in a new area, the planner would have control over the number of models depending upon the resources available. Quite often the very nature of the project will indicate the number of models necessary. For example if a livestock project involves different groups of farms to produce beef, milk, eggs, broilers, and pork, it would be necessary to design a separate model for each component. Or if the sizes or the income levels are significantly different in each group of farms, separate models would be necessary to reflect not only the various kinds of production, but also the different levels of management. Then if each farm combines different kinds of enterprises, it would be necessary to design enough models to reflect the combination of enterprises according to the size of the operation and the type of management.

The preparation of models is perhaps the most important feature in planning agricultural projects. Each model embodies the assumptions about the productive capacity of the farms it represents. The data for each model are arranged in the form of the various budgets discussed in earlier chapters. The budget for land shows what and how much can be produced; the labor budget shows whether family labor will be adequate for the production program and what additional labor might be hired; the budget for physical resources indicates the inputs required for the project. Based on these budgets, the budget for financial resources can be prepared, and the financial analysis for each model can be undertaken.

In preparing the financial analysis for each model, a crucial task is projecting production over the life of the project. Projecting crop production, which is usually related to the land area, is quite straightforward. Projecting livestock production, which is related to the number of the producing units and their productive capacity, is sometimes more difficult.

Crop Projections

The World Bank's Tamil Nadu agricultural credit project in India[1] provides a good example of the use of crop production models in project

1. World Bank, "Tamil Nadu Agricultural Credit Project—India," PA-81a (a restricted-circulation document) (Washington, D.C., 1971).

analysis. This project was designed to enable farmers in two main geographic regions to invest in minor schemes for irrigation, land leveling, drainage, and mechanization. The first region, consisting of the coastal plain with sedimentary soils, has an average annual rainfall of about 200 millimeters (8 inches); the second region, a central plateau mainly with red soils on crystalline rock formations, has about 800 millimeters of rain. The type of irrigation development, which was one of the project's main elements, depended on the geology. Filter points and tubewells were concentrated in the areas of sedimentary soils; dugwells (or open wells), in the areas of crystalline rock. Land was leveled only within the command areas of surface irrigation schemes, where water could be controlled and distributed evenly. Farm mechanization was introduced in certain areas for faster and more timely cultivation and higher cropping intensities.

Six models were designed, representing the different soil structures and the various kinds of investments in the project. Model I: investment in filter point on five-hectare farms with sedimentary soils in the Cauvery Delta; model II: shallow tubewell on ten-hectare farms in a sedimentary area of South Arcot; model III: medium tubewell on ten-hectare farms in a crystalling rock area; model IV: energized dugwell on five-hectare farms in a crystalling rock area; model V: land-leveling on five-hectare farms with black-cotton soils; and model VI: medium-size tractor with implements on fifteen-hectare farms with full irrigation in a crystalling area.

Table 6–1 shows the crop area and yield for each of these models, both without the project and at its full development. This table provides further justification for the preparation of the separate models, because the essential features vary a great deal, whether in terms of the kinds of crops grown, the area devoted to each, the cropping intensity, or the levels of yield. Only models I and II were growing similar crops, but the area for each crop in model II was twice that in model I. Only model III had chillies, and only model IV included sorghum. Sugarcane was introduced with the development program in the model V farm. In model VI the area devoted to sugarcane was expanded in the program.

In preparing farm models, the analyst should be careful to reflect what the farmer is likely to do, not what he should do. Especially when planning for semisubsistence farms, the strong interdependence between the farm and the home and its effect on decisionmaking should always be remembered. If cropping programs are changed, new crops are introduced, or new practices are to be adopted, it must be remembered that adjustment takes time and that people adapt at different rates. These rates are affected by the nature of the change, the family's needs for cash, the farmer's skills, his expectations about markets, the availability of inputs, or the effectiveness of the extension program. In general, the time needed to introduce

Table 6–1. *Crop Area and Yield for the Tamil Nadu Farm Models*

	Area (hectares)		Yield (tons per hectare)	
Model	Without project	Full development	Without project	Full development
I. Filter point				
1st crop paddy	1.0	2.5	2.5	3.2
2nd crop paddy	1.0	2.0	2.0	2.6
Single crop paddy	2.5	1.0	2.5	3.0
Pulses	0.5	0.5	0.4	0.6
Maize	0.5	0.5	2.0	5.0
Cotton (seed)	...	0.5	...	1.0
Total	5.5	7.0	—	—
Cropping intensity (percentage)	110	140	—	—
II. Shallow tubewell				
1st crop paddy	2.0	5.0	2.5	3.2
2nd crop paddy	2.0	4.0	2.0	2.6
Single crop paddy	5.0	2.0	2.5	3.0
Pulses	1.0	1.0	0.4	0.6
Maize	1.0	1.0	2.0	5.0
Cotton (seed)	...	1.0	...	1.0
Total	11.0	14.0	—	—
Cropping intensity (percentage)	110	140	—	—
III. Medium tubewell				
Maize	2.0	3.0	2.0	5.0
Pulses	3.0	2.0	0.4	0.6
Oilseeds	2.0	3.0	0.8	1.2
Chillies	...	1.0	...	1.2
Paddy	...	3.0	1.5	2.6
Total	7.0	12.0	—	—
Cropping intensity (percentage)	70	120	—	—
IV. Energized dugwell				
Sorghum	1.0	2.0	0.8	3.0
Oilseeds	1.5	2.0	0.8	1.2
Pulses	1.0	1.0	0.4	0.6
Paddy	...	1.0	...	2.6
Total	3.5	6.0	—	—
Cropping intensity (percentage)	70	120	—	—

Table 6–1 (continued)

Model	Area (hectares)		Yield (tons per hectare)	
	Without project	Full development	Without project	Full development
V. Land-leveling				
Pulses	2.0	1.0	0.4	0.6
Paddy	1.0	1.0	2.0	2.5
Oilseeds	...	1.0	...	1.2
Cotton (seed)	1.0	2.0	0.5	1.0
Sugar cane	...	1.0	...	100.0
Total	4.0	6.0	—	—
Cropping intensity (percentage)	80	120	—	—
VI. Medium-size tractor with implements				
Pulses	2.0	1.5	0.65	0.65
Paddy	6.0	8.0	2.8	2.8
Maize	2.0	3.0	4.5	5.1
Oilseeds	3.0	3.0	1.2	1.3
Cotton (seed)	2.0	3.0	1.0	1.1
Sugar cane	3.0	4.0	95.0	105.0
Total	18.0	22.5	—	—
Cropping intensity (percentage)	120	150	—	—

... Zero or negligible.
— Not applicable.
Source: Adapted from World Bank, "Tamil Nadu Agricultural Credit Project—India."

a new crop is longer than that needed to improve old crops familiar to the farmer. Permanent tree crops with long maturation periods will take longer to reach full development than short-term crops. Similarly, crops susceptible to pests and diseases are delicate to manage and will require more time to reach full development than more resistant crops. The full effect of changing a rotation program, introducing an irrigation scheme, or bringing additional land under cultivation cannot be felt fully until several production seasons have elapsed. In certain projects, total production may even decline for a time as farmers adjust to the new crop or to new practices, or as land is taken out of production in the changeover process.

Two critical indexes that express the rate of adjustment are projections for the land area to be brought into the project each year and projections for yields. Projecting the land area to be improved each year is relatively simple; it depends on the resources of the project staff and assumptions about the farmers' rate of adaption. Projecting yields, which are influenced by the interaction of many factors, is far more difficult. Some of these factors are physical and biological; others are affected by human behavior. Because of the variety of these influences, a wide range of yield levels may exist even within a particular area that has a uniform basic factor, such as soil type.

Projecting yield levels even one year in advance is a difficult proposition, so the problems of making projections over the life of the project can be well imagined. Three pitfalls, in particular, should be avoided: (a) assuming that current yields will remain unchanged during the life of the project; (b) using unadjusted data derived from experimental stations; and (c) projecting future yield by extrapolating past trends.

The assumption that yields will remain unchanged during the life of the project could introduce fallacies. The first fallacy presumes that yields have already reached the maximum levels and cannot be increased by introducing new technology or other improvements in the project, thus underestimating the effects of the project. The second fallacy assumes that conditions in the project area could not deteriorate if the project were not implemented, thus underestimating the value of the project. The third assumes that productivity in the area could not possibly be improved without the project, thus overstating the benefits of the project. Clearly each situation must be judged on its own merits and models should be constructed to reflect the changes in productivity with and without the project. Then the incremental benefit expected from the project's implementation can be assessed as accurately as possible.

Unadjusted data from experimental stations are misleading because these stations are operated under conditions that approximate the ideal. Farmers rarely, if ever, achieve the same results. Some analysts think that the maximum to be achieved under field conditions is from 50 to 60 percent of the results from experimental stations. Results from demonstration farms in the project area are closer to real life; nevertheless, these farms often receive considerably more care and attention from the farmer and extension officer than do crops in normal field conditions.

If the analyst projects future yield by simply extrapolating past trends, he has failed to consider the effect of new technology or improved practices that may be introduced. Although previous levels of performance should be considered when estimating new yield levels and the rate of the expected increase, changes brought about by the project must be accounted for.

It is particularly difficult to project yields for a new crop introduced into an area because there is no previous local experience to draw on. One solution is to arrange for yield trials on experimental stations and demonstration plots under various conditions within the project area, but this is feasible only for short-term crops. Long-term crops take too long to yield useful data. The analyst often has to draw on the experience of farmers or experimental farms in other areas or countries where the crop has been grown under conditions similar to those in the project area. These experiences must then be related to the particular characteristics of the project area, the ability of the extension staff to transmit the new technology, and the readiness of the farmers to accept it.

Table 6–2 illustrates the projection of yields using data from the World Bank's Second Atlantico project in Colombia.[2] Projections for sorghum, sesame, maize, and cotton—the traditional crops grown in the area—were based on previous yields. Soybeans, groundnuts, and tomatoes were the new crops. Their yields were based on trials in the project, as well as on yields obtained by farmers under comparable dry farming conditions in the area.

Table 6–2. *Projection of Yields for the Second Atlantico Development Project*
(tons per hectare)

Crop	Year				
	1	2	3	4	5
Sorghum	2.40	2.70	2.85	3.00	3.00
Sesame	0.56	0.63	0.67	0.70	0.70
Maize	2.00	2.25	2.38	2.50	2.50
Cotton (seed cotton)	1.26	1.44	1.62	1.71	1.80
Soybeans	1.44	1.62	1.71	1.80	1.80
Groundnuts (unshelled)	1.12	1.28	1.44	1.52	1.60
Tomato	10.50	12.00	13.50	14.25	15.00

Source: Adapted from World Bank, "Second Atlantico Development Project—Colombia."

Table 6–3 shows the percentage increase in yield over the base period (year 1) calculated for each year of the project. The potential for improvement in sorghum, sesame, and maize was less than that for the new crops, and they reached maximum production in a shorter time. The new crops, such as groundnuts, take longer to attain full potential. So do the more labor-intensive, high-valued crops, such as cotton and tomatoes, which require more time for the farmer to adapt to new techniques and to rigorous managerial requirements.[3]

2. World Bank, "Second Atlantico Development Project—Colombia," PA-846 (a restricted-circulation document) (Washington, D.C., 1972), Annex 15, Table 4.

3. B. F. Stanton, "Second Atlantico Project (Colombia) Case Study on Preparing Budgets for a Period of Years," EDI course material, AC–111–S (Washington, D.C.: World Bank, 1972; processed).

Table 6–3. *Increase in Yield for the Second Atlantico Development Project*

Crop	Year			
	2	3	4	5
Sorghum	12.5	19.0	25.0	25.0
Sesame	12.5	19.6	25.0	25.0
Maize	12.5	19.0	25.0	25.0
Cotton (seed cotton)	14.2	28.6	35.7	42.9
Soybeans	12.5	19.0	25.0	25.0
Groundnuts (unshelled)	14.2	28.6	35.7	42.9
Tomato	14.2	28.6	35.7	42.9

Source: Same as for Table 6–2.

In the five models prepared for this project, the analysts assumed the same basic projection of yields. This assumption is not always valid. Differences in characteristics are likely to be reflected in the level and rate of increase in yield. As a general rule each model should be treated independently, and separate yield projections should be made for each.

Projecting yields is perhaps one of the most difficult, yet most important, areas of project analysis. Assumptions about the level and the rate of increase in yield will influence the flows of incremental benefits accruing from the project.

Livestock Projections

Projections of production from livestock enterprises are related to the number of livestock, which is not necessarily related to land area. Unlike land, which is merely a producing unit, livestock are reproducing (breeding) as well as producing units.

Livestock projects may consist of only breeding operations, only producing operations, or both. Breeding operations involve the production of offspring on a farm from animals reared on that farm. Producing operations involve the rearing of animals for final consumption or sale, or the production of livestock products from animals reared but not born on the farm, for example, the fattening of purchased pigs and cattle, or the production of broiler meat and eggs from fertile eggs not produced on the farm. The production of weaners for sale would be regarded as a breeding operation. But if some of the weaners were retained for fattening on the farm, it would be a producing and breeding operation.

For purely producing operations, total production of the commodity being produced is based on the average yield per animal. Where breeding operations are involved, it is necessary to determine the herd or flock composition expected on the farm each year. This is calculated by estimating the parent's reproductive capability on the basis of family history and managerial practices on the farm. Appropriate yield levels are then applied to the various categories of producing operations on the farm to determine total production each year.

A few examples drawn from the appraisal of a livestock project in the Philippines[4] illustrate the principles underlying livestock projections. It was a complex project that included proposals for financing the expansion of egg, broiler, and pig production; the construction of slaughterhouses; and beef production on large hill farms and on coconut farms of different sizes. The project was divided into nine components with separate models prepared for each. The four discussed in this study are broiler production, egg production, beef cattle fattening, and integrated coconut and cattle breeding and fattening.

Broiler production

Table 6–4 shows the flock projection for the broiler component of the project. The objective of this component is to increase broiler capacity on 250 farms from 4,000 to 8,000 birds. The model is simple, because it only involves the production of broiler meat from day-old chicks purchased from hatcheries. The technical coefficients in the table give the basic assumption of the projections. They indicate that chicks are purchased at one day old and sold after eight weeks, that five batches are technically feasible during the average year, and that the mortality rate is 5 percent. Since allowance must be made for the construction of buildings to accommodate the additional 4,000 birds per batch, it is assumed that, in the first year of the project, five batches will be obtained from the original housing and only four from the new. From year 2 to the end of the project, five batches will be produced annually.

Without the project, 20,000 chicks are paid for, but 20,400 are supplied

4. World Bank, "Appraisal of the Second Livestock Development Project—Philippines," 1070-PH (a restricted-circulation document) (Washington, D.C., 1976). These examples are based on a preparation report submitted by the Development Bank of Philippines (DBP) and appraised by a World Bank mission to the Philippines from April 18 to May 22, 1975. The staff of the DBP and all mission members (Anthony J. Blackwood, M. J. Walshe, D. I. Sillar, E. W. Root, Maxwell L. Brown, and Dominique J. Babelon) contributed to the preparation of the original model.

Table 6–4. *Flock Projection in Broiler Production Model*

Item	Without project	With project (year)	
		1	2–10
Flock composition			
Broilers (0–8 weeks)	4,000	8,000	8,000
Purchases			
Day-old chicks paid for	20,000	36,000	40,000
Day-old chicks delivered[a]	20,400	36,720	40,800
Mortality			
Broilers (0–8 weeks)	1,020	1,836	2,040
Sales			
Broilers	19,380	34,884	38,760
Technical coefficients			
Age at purchase (days)	1	1	1
Age at sale (weeks)	8	8	8
Batches per year (number)	5	5/4[b]	5
Mortality (percentage)	5	5	5

a. An extra 2 percent of purchased chicks are supplied free of cost.
b. This represents five batches in the old houses and four batches in the new during year 1.
Sources: Adapted from World Bank, "Appraisal of the Second Livestock Project—Philippines."

each year, the difference being a 2 percent provision to cover losses on delivery. In the first year of the project 36,720 chicks are to be supplied. From the second year to the close of the project, 40,800 are to be supplied each year. On the assumption of a 5 percent mortality, sales are expected to be 19,380 each year without the project, 34,884 in year 1 of the project, and 38,760 in each of the following years until the end of the project.

The flock composition shows the size of each batch at full capacity. It is assumed that the first batch is purchased at the beginning of the year and that the last batch is sold before the end of the year. Thus, there will be no inventory of birds at the end of each year and at the end of the project.

Egg production

The objective of this component is to increase the capacity of the laying flock on 150 farms from 2,000 to 6,000 birds. The model assumes that:

(a) Day-old chicks will be purchased;
(b) They will grow into layers in six months;
(c) The layers will be productive for eighteen months, after which they will be sold as culls;

(d) On the average, 60 percent of the hens will be laying each day over the life of the project;

(e) The mortality of chicks and growers will be 11 percent of the number of chicks purchased; and

(f) The mortality of layers will be 23.5 percent of the average annual size of the laying flock, except in year 2, when the size is in a state of transition.

This model introduces a few elements not encountered in the broiler production model. The broiler model assumes that broilers are produced in five discrete batches each year; this model assumes continuous production. In the broiler model, the baby chicks grow into broilers, which then are sold as the final output of the project; in the egg production model, the baby chicks grow into layers, which then produce table eggs as the final output, thus adding a second stage in the production process.

The flock projection in Table 6–5 may be more easily understood with the help of the flow chart in Table 6–6. There are four laying houses at different stages of production on the farm. The numbers in the chart represent the number of birds at six month intervals. The chart covers the period extending from two years before the beginning of the project (B_2 and B_1) to the end of the ten year project. The entries for house 1 show that 750 chicks are purchased at the beginning of B_2. After allowing for 11 percent chick mortality, 667 chicks survive to the time at which they begin to lay eggs. Mortality of another 200 birds, representing 30 percent of the surviving chicks, is assumed to be evenly distributed over the eighteen month laying period. At the end of two years, the remaining 467 birds in the house are culled, and a new batch of chicks is purchased. At this point the project begins. But house 1 is not ready to accommodate an increased number of birds until facilities have been expanded. So, another 750 chicks are purchased. This pattern is followed in the other three houses, but each starts the cycle half a year later than another. When house 2 is ready to take in a new batch of chicks in the middle of year 1, facilities have been expanded to accommodate 2,250 birds.

At the end of B_1, just before the project starts, flock composition consists of 667 pullets which will begin to lay eggs in house 4, and altogether 1,133 layers in houses 2 (533) and 3 (600). The average size of the laying flock at the beginning of the project is 1,700. This is found by calculating the average number of layers on the farm during the preceding twelve months. In house 1 the average is 533; in house 2, 600. In house 3, the laying period starts in the latter half of the year, whereas in house 4 it extends only to the first half of the year. To obtain the average number of layers for the whole year in these two houses, the average number of birds in house 3 during the last six months of the year (633) is added to

Table 6–5. *Flock Projection in Egg Production Model*

Item	Without project	With project (year)		
		1	2	3–10
Flock composition at end of year				
Point-of-lay birds	667	2,000	2,000	2,000
Layers	1,133	1,133	3,400	3,400
Total	1,800	3,133	5,400	5,400
Average annual laying flock	1,700	1,700	3,533	5,100
Purchases				
Day-old chicks	1,500	3,000	4,500	4,500
Mortality				
Chicks and growers	166	333	500	500
Layers	400	400	800	1,200
Total mortality	566	733	1,300	1,700
Sales				
Culled birds	934	934	934	2,800
Eggs	372,300	372,300	773,727	1,116,900
Technical coefficients				
Age at purchase (days)	1	1	1	1
Laying period (months)	18	18	18	18
Age at sale (years)	2	2	2	2
Average percentage of hens laying per day	60	60	60	60
Mortality				
Chicks and growers (percentage of chicks bought)	11	11	11	11
Layers (percentage of average annual laying flock[a])	23.5	23.5	22.6[b]	23.5

a. Mortality includes layers that are removed from the flock before normal culling, because it would be uneconomic to keep them. It is calculated at the rate of 30 percent of the surviving chicks distributed evenly over the eighteen-month laying period.

b. In year 2 the size of the laying flock would be in a state of transition.

Source: Same as for Table 6–4.

the average in house 4 during the first six months (500); the sum is then divided by 2, resulting in 567 layers.

The number of eggs produced each day can be calculated by multiplying the average annual size of the laying flock by the percentage of the hens laying each day. Annual production is obtained by multiplying daily production by 365, the number of days in the year. For example, at full

Table 6–6. *Flock Projection in Egg Production Model (Flowchart)*

House number	Without project		With project (year)			
	B₂	B₁	1	2	3	4–10
1	467** / 750* 667	600 533 / 750* 467**	667 600	533	467** / 2,250* 2,000	1,800 1,600 / 1,400**
2	533 / 467**	750* 667 / 600 533	2,250* 2,000 / 467**	1,800 1,600	1,400** / 2,250* 2,000	1,800 1,600
3	600 533 / 467**	750* 667 / 600	2,250* 2,000 / 467**	1,800 1,600	1,400** / 2,250* 2,000	1,600
4	667 600 533 / 467**	750* 667	2,250* 2,000 / 467**	1,800 1,600	2,250* 2,000	2,000

Notes: - - - - = growing period; ——— = laying period; * number of day-old chicks bought; ** number sold as culls.
Source: Same as for Table 6–4.

81

production from the year 3 to end of the project, the annual egg production is 1,116,900, calculated as:

$$5,100 \times 0.60 \times 365 = 1,116,900 \text{ eggs.}$$

Beef cattle fattening

Table 6–7 presents herd projections in a simple model for a small beef cattle fattening operation. In this component, an existing five hectare coconut plantation will begin to rear cattle as an additional enterprise. The first year of the project will be devoted to developing the pasture. The farm's carrying capacity will reach 1.4 animal units per hectare by the second year, providing pasture for seven animal units on the five hectares. The farmer will then purchase seven feeder cattle weighing approximately 150 kilograms each. Making an average liveweight gain of 400 grams a head each day, these animals are to be sold in the following year at an average liveweight of 300 kilograms. In the third year, the total carrying capacity will increase to eight animal units. Eight feeder steers will be

Table 6–7. *Herd Production in Beef Cattle Fattening Model*

Item	Without project	With project (year)				
		1	2	3	4	5–20
Herd composition at end of year						
Feeder cattle 1 to 2 years	...	...	7	8	8	8
Animal units	...	...	7	8	8	8
Purchases						
Feeder cattle 1 to 2 years	...	...	7	8	8	8
Mortality						
Feeder cattle 1 to 2 years	...	...	0	0	0	0
Sales						
Fattened cattle 2 to 3 years	...	...	0	7	8	8
Technical coefficients						
Purchase liveweight (kilograms)	—	—	150	150	150	150
Selling liveweight (kilograms)	—	—	300	300	300	300
Liveweight gain (grams/head/day)	—	—	400	400	400	400
Average fattening period (months)	—	—	12.5	12.5	12.5	12.5
Carrying capacity (animal units per hectare)	—	—	1.4	1.6	1.6	1.6
Total carrying capacity (animal units)	—	—	7	8	8	8

... Zero or negligible.
— Not applicable.
Source: Same as for Table 6–4.

Table 6–8. *Conversion Ratio for Cattle*

Kind of livestock	Animal unit
Used by the U.S. Department of Agriculture	
1 Milk cow	1.00
1 Beef cow	0.75
1 Cattle on feed	0.74
1 Other dairy cattle	0.44
1 Other beef cattle	0.34
Used by the Farm Economics Branch, School of Agriculture, Cambridge University, United Kingdom	
Dairy cows, 11-cwt animal, giving 350 gallons at 3.75 B.F.	1.00
Dairy cows, 11-cwt animal, giving 650 gallons at 3.75 B.F.	1.25
Dairy cows, 11-cwt animal, giving 1,000 gallons at 3.75 B.F.	1.50
Other cattle, 2 year old, 9 cwt, gaining 1 pound liveweight per day	1.00
Other cattle, 1½ year old, 7 cwt, gaining 1 pound of liveweight per day	0.75
Other cattle, 1 year old, 5 cwt, gaining 1 pound liveweight per day	0.67
Other cattle, ½–1 year old, gaining 1 pound liveweight per day	0.50
Other cattle, 0–½ year old, gaining 1 pound liveweight per day	0.25
Used by the U. K. Ministry of Agriculture, Fisheries, and Food	
Dairy cows	1
Beef cows	1
Other cattle	
2 years and over	1
1 to 2 years	2/3
under 1 year	1/3

Sources: For U.S.D.A. and Cambridge University methods: Yang, *Methods of Farm Management Investigations.* For U.K. Ministry method: United Kingdom Ministry of Agriculture, Fisheries and Food, *The Farm as a Business.*

purchased, fattened, and then sold in year 4. Since the number of animals is small, mortality is assumed to be negligible and therefore is ignored. A more conservative approach would allow for one animal dying about every four or five years.

The herd composition in Table 6–7 shows the number of animals on the farm at the end of each year. This number is converted to animal units in order to aggregate animals at different stages of production. Unfortu-

Table 6–9. *Herd Projection for Cattle Breeding and Fattening Model*

Item	With project (years)							
	1	2	3	4	5	6	7	8–20
Herd compostition at end of year								
Bulls	1	1	1	1	1	1	1	1
Breeding cows and replacements	9	28	25	25	26	27	27	27
Calves weaned	0	5	17	11	12	12	12	12
Heifers, 1–2 years	0	0	3	5	5	4	4	4
Steers, 1–2 years	0	0	8	8	6	8	8	8
Total number of animals	10	34	54	50	50	52	52	52
Total animal units	10	29	37	39	38	40	40	40
Purchases								
Bulls	1	0	0	0	1	0	0	0
Heifers, 1–2 years	9	19	0	0	0	0	0	0
Steers, 1–2 years	0	0	8	0	0	0	0	0
Total	10	19	8	0	1	0	0	0
Mortality								
Bulls	0	0	0	0	0	0	0	0
Breeding cows and replacements	0	0	1	0	1	1	1	1
Heifers, 1–2 years	0	0	0	0	0	0	0	0
Steers, 1–2 years	0	0	0	0	0	0	0	0
Total mortality	0	0	1	0	1	1	1	1
Sales								
Cull bulls	0	0	0	0	1	0	0	0
Cull cows	0	0	2	3	3	3	3	3
Calves weaned	0	0	0	5	6	7	8	8
Steers, 1–2 years	0	0	2	0	0	0	0	0
Steers, 2–3 years	0	0	0	8	8	6	8	8
Heifers, 1–2 years	0	0	0	4	0	0	0	0
Total sales	0	0	4	20	18	16	19	19
Technical coefficients								
Calves weaned (percentage)	—	60	60	65	70	75	75	75
Mortality, adult (percentage)	—	2	2	2	2	2	2	2
Cull rate, breeders (percentage)	—	5	7	10	12	12	12	12
Cull rate, bulls (percentage)	—	20	20	20	20	20	20	20
Carrying capacity (animal unit)	10	30	40	40	40	40	40	40
Area improved (hectare)	10	20	20	20	20	20	20	20

— Not applicable.
Source: Same as for Table 6–4.

nately, the measurement of animal units is not standardized. It is generally defined as the equivalent of a mature breeding cow, but other ratios are also used. Yang's study on farm management quotes two sets of ratios: one used by the U.S. Department of Agriculture and the other by the Cambridge University's Farm Economics Branch in the United Kingdom and reported in the 1955 edition of the *Farm as a Business*.[5] The 1958 edition of *The Farm as a Business*[6] reports another set of ratios. The different standards are compared in Table 6–8. In the World Bank's cattle projects, for the sake of simplicity one animal unit is assigned to animals one year or older, but those that are younger are ignored.

Cattle breeding and fattening.

Table 6–9 presents a more complicated model that combines breeding and fattening on a twenty hectare coconut farm. The technical coefficients in the table specify the assumptions underlying the projection for herd composition, purchases, deaths, and sales. During the first year of the project, one bull and nine pregnant heifers are purchased. These numbers are entered in the herd composition (one bull; nine breeding cows and replacements) at the end of year 1. During the second year, nineteen additional pregnant heifers are purchased, bringing the number of breeding cows and replacements to twenty-eight at the end of year 2.

Starting from the second year, calves are weaned each year. The number weaned in each year is calculated by multiplying the weaning percentage in that year by the number of breeding females in the herd at the beginning of the year (or the end of the previous year). For example, there are nine breeding cows and replacements in the herd at the end of year 1; the weaning percentage in year 2 is 60 percent. So the number of calves weaned in year 2 is obtained by multiplying nine by 60 percent; the result is five. The number of calves weaned in year 3 is calculated in the same way (that is, $28 \times 0.60 = 17$).

Weaned calves are assumed to be divided equally between steers and heifers. Where there is an odd number of calves, the odd one is allocated to heifers and steers alternately. Thus, the five calves weaned in year 2 are divided into three heifers and two steers in year 3. The three heifers remain in the herd at the end of the year, whereas the two steers are sold during the year.

5. W. Y. Yang, *Methods of Farm Management Investigations* (Rome: Food and Agricultural Organization, 1965), p. 60.

6. United Kingdom Ministry of Agriculture, Fisheries, and Food, *The Farm as a Business* (London: Her Majesty's Stationery Office, 1958), p. 44.

Two culled cows are also sold during year 3. The number of culled cows is obtained by multiplying the culling rate of breeders for the year by the number of breeding females at the beginning of the year 4, after allowing for mortality. Thus, at the mortality rate of 2 percent in year 3, one out of the twenty-eight breeders at the end of year 2 dies in year 3. Then, at the culling rate of 7 percent for year 3, two out of the twenty-seven surviving breeding females are culled, as entered in the table under the sales items for year 3. This convention of allowing for mortality before calculating the number of culls is not adopted by some analysts.

The size of the farm is twenty hectares, of which ten are improved in year 1 to carry ten animal units. All twenty hectares are improved to carry thirty animal units in year 2 and forty in year 3. Eight steers are purchased in year 3 to utilize the additional pasture. This brings the total number of animals to fifty-four at the end of year 3. Following the World Bank convention, calves are ignored in calculating the number of animal units. Thus, the number of animal units at the end of year 3 is thirty-seven.

At a weaning rate of 65 percent for year 4, the twenty-five cows in the herd at the end of year 3 wean sixteen calves in year 4. Five weaned calves are sold, and eleven remain in the herd at the end of year 4. The seventeen calves in the herd at the end of year 3 are assumed to comprise eight steers and nine heifers. The eight steers remain in the herd at the end of year 4. Four heifers are regarded as surplus and sold, and the other five are retained for herd expansion. These are shown as "heifers, 1–2 years" in the herd composition at the end of year 4. The three heifers in the herd at the end of year 3 are added to the number of breeding cows and replacements in the herd at the end of year 4. The total number of breeding cows and replacements at the end of year 4 is calculated as shown below.[7]

Step		Number of cattle
Herd composition at end of year 3	=	25
minus Mortality (2 percent of 25)	=	1
		24
minus Culls (10 percent of 24)	=	2
		22
plus Heifers at the end of year 3 transferred to breeding herd	=	3
Herd composition at the end of year 4	=	25

7. Adapted from World Bank, "Appraisal of the Second Livestock Development Project—Philippines."

The model achieves stability in year 7. Thereafter the number of animals leaving each category is offset by the number entering that category, and all the elements within the model remain constant. For example, sales remain constant, with three cull cows, eight weaners, and eight steers sold each year. The composition of the herd remains constant with the same number of animals in each category. And the number of animal units remains constant at forty, which is the maximum that can be accommodated on the farm.

The general process for calculating the number of a given category of animals in the herd at the end of a year is shown below.

(1)   Balance from end of previous year;
(2)   *minus* Mortality, calculated as a percentage of (1);
(3)   *minus* Culls, calculated as a percentage of (1) − (2);
(4)   *minus* Other sales (besides culls);
(5)   *minus* Transfers to other categories in the herd;
(6)   *plus* Transfers from herd sources;
(7)   *plus* Purchases or gifts;
(8)   *equals* Balance at the end of year.

Table 6–10 illustrates this process with the calculations for the herd composition at the end of the project's eighth year.

Table 6–10. *Number of Cattle at the End of Year 8*

Step		Number of cattle
Bulls		
Balance at the end of year 7		1
minus Mortality (2 percent of 1)		0
	=	1
minus Culls (20 percent of 1) + sales		0
	=	1
plus Purchases		0
Balance at end of year 8	=	1
Breeding cows and replacements		
Balance at end of year 7		27
minus Mortality (2 percent of 27)		1
	=	26
minus Culls (12 percent of 26)		3
	=	23
plus Heifers at the end of year 7		4
Balance at the end of year 8	=	27

(table continued on the following page)

Table 6–10 (*continued*)

Step		Number of cattle
Calves weaned		
Balance at the end of year 7		12
minus Transfers wihin herd		12
	=	0
plus 75 percent of breeding cows and replacements at the end of year 7		20
minus Weaners sold (male 2, female 6)		8
Balance at the end of year 8	=	12
Heifers, 1–2 years		
Balance at the end of year 7		4
minus Mortality (2 percent of 4)		0
	=	4
minus Transfer to breeding herd		4
	=	0
plus Transfers from calves weaned at the end of year 7		4
Balance at the end of year 8	=	4
Steers, 1–2 years		
Balance at the end of year 7		8
minus Mortality (2 percent of 8)		0
	=	8
minus Sales		8
	=	0
plus Transfers from calves weaned of year 7		8
Balance at the end of year 8		8

Source: Same as for Table 6–4.

A formula has been developed by Gittinger to calculate the composition of the stable herd at full development based on the number of cows in the herd at the beginning of the year (x), and given the number of animals in the herd, the technical coefficients for calving, mortality, and the ratio of bulls to cows. It is used in the Kitulo Ranch herd build-up and stabilization exercise,[8] which assumes the following technical coefficients at full development.

8. J. Price Gittinger and Janet K. Stockard, "Kitulo Plateau Ranch Herd Build-up and Stabilization Exercise," EDI course material, AE-1066-P&S (Washington, D.C.: World Bank, 1974; processed).

Coefficient	Value
Calves weaned	80 percent
Mortality	3 percent
Survival rate	97 percent
Culling rates:	
Bulls	20 percent
Breeding cows	12 percent
Heifers, 2–3 years	10 percent
Bulls as a percentage of breeding females	3 percent
Size of ranch	9,200 hectares
Stocking rate (animal units per hectare)	0.98
Carrying capacity (animal units)	9,016

Using Gittinger's method for calculating the herd composition, the following equation is solved for X, the number of cows:

$$\underset{\text{Cows}}{X} + \underset{\text{Bulls}}{0.03X} + \underset{\substack{\text{Heifers,} \\ \text{1–2 years}}}{0.97\left(\frac{0.8}{2}\right)X} + \underset{\substack{\text{Steers,} \\ \text{1–2 years}}}{0.97\left(\frac{0.8}{2}\right)X} + \underset{\substack{\text{Steers,} \\ \text{2–3 years}}}{(0.97)(0.97)\left(\frac{0.8}{2}\right)X} = \underset{\substack{\text{Animal} \\ \text{units}}}{9,016}$$

$$X = 4,132$$

The composition of the herd at full development then is obtained by substituting the value of X in the equation to obtain:

Kind of cattle	Number of cattle
Breeding cows and	
replacements	4,132
Bulls	124
Heifers, 1–2 years	1,603
Steers, 1–2 years	1,603
Steers, 2–3 years	1,555
Total animal units	9,016

In the *Kitulo case*, the two-to-three year old steers are assumed to be sold during the course of the year, but they are included in the herd composition at the end of the year as though they were all sold on the last day of the year. Although this approach somewhat overstates the actual use of the grazing area, it serves as a conservative measure to ensure that grazing facilities are always adequate.

By contrast, the methodology adopted in Table 6–9 does not include in the herd composition for the end of the year the two-to-three year old steers sold during the year. The justifications are that the herd is small and that the carrying capacity of pastures has been conservatively estimated to allow for adequate pasture facilities. This is a reasonable approach in making projections for a small herd, but for a large herd, the approach adopted in the Kitulo case is recommended.

For a dairy herd, or for a dual-purpose herd that produces milk and beef for sale, the same principles used in the beef breeding and fattening model are used in herd projections. Since milk production is determined by the number and productivity of lactating cows, however, the technical coefficients should include assumptions about the calving percentage and the average yield for lactating cows over the life of the project.

7

•·•··•··•·•··•··•·•··•··•·•··•··•·•··•··•·•··•··•·•··•··•·•··•··•·•··•··•·•··•··•·•··•··•·•··•··•·•··•··•·•··•··•·•··•··•·•··•··•·•··•··•·•··•··•·•··•··•·•··•·

Financial Analysis

The financial analysis is that phase of project analysis in which a project's viability is assessed from the viewpoint of the individuals or agencies contributing capital and sharing its rewards.[1] Since the method of analysis for the farm family is similar to that for any of the other participants, only the preparation of the financial analysis for the farm family is discussed. It is often necessary to prepare separate financial analyses, however, for the treasury, credit institutions, cooperatives, marketing boards, or other agencies that help to finance the project or that provide services. Indeed, the results of such analysis can have important implications for the success of the project and for the viability of the particular entity.

The financial analysis for the farm family can be approached from two angles: by calculating the rate of return on the farm family's own investment, and by calculating the rate of return on all the capital invested in the project. The rate of return on the farm family's capital is calculated after all the capital provided by financial sources outside of the farm family is accounted for. Therefore the receipt of loans and the costs for debt service must be included in the analysis. This rate of return could be called the rate of return after financing. To calculate the rate of return on the total capital invested in the project, receipt of loans and the costs for debt service must be excluded. This rate of return can be described as the rate

---

1. The term financial analysis sometimes refers to projection of funds flows, ratio analysis, and other types of analysis that yield information about the financial viability, the efficiency of management, and the past and projected performance of a firm. See Jack L. Upper and Janet K. Stockard, "Introduction to a Funds Flow Approach to Project Analysis," EDI course material, CN–18 (Washington, D.C.: World Bank, 1977; processed).

Table 7-1. *Format for Financial Analysis, after Financing*

Item	Without project	With project (year)		
		1	2	3
(a) Inflows				
Gross value of production				
Loan receipts				
Grants				
Rental value of farmhouse				
Salvage or residual value				
Other[a]				
Total				
(b) Outflows				
Investment (farm development) costs				
Cash operating expenses				
Hired labor paid in kind				
Debt service				
Interest				
Repayment of principal				
Other				
Total				
(c) Farm family net benefit[b] (a) − (b)				
(d) Farm family net benefit without project[c]				
(e) Incremental family net benefit (cash flow)[d] (c) − (d)				

Financial rate of return on the farm family's capital = ＿＿ percent

a. Other inflows would include items such as revenue from hiring out equipment.
b. Includes compensation for (a) capital existing without the project; (b) owned land; (c) family labor and management; and (d) new capital invested in the project.
c. Includes compensation for (a) capital existing without the project; (b) owned land; and (c) family labor and management.
d. Includes (d) compensation for new capital invested in the project only.

of return before financing. These two financial rates of return can be presented in separate tables or combined in a single table. Table 7-1 presents a format for the direct approach in calculating the financial rate of return after financing; Table 7-9 illustrates the use of the alternative approach.

As shown in Table 7-1, the main items involved in preparing the financial analysis are inflows, outflows, farm family net benefit, farm family net benefit without the project, and incremental farm family net benefit. Inflows are positive resource flows that enhance the attractiveness of the project. They include the gross value of production, loan receipts, grants, subsidies, and the rental value of the farm. Outflows are negative resource flows. They represent the resources used up to create the project output. Included under outflows are investment costs for farm development, cash operating expenses, hired labor paid in kind, and debt service (when financing requirements are considered). Each of these items is discussed below.

Gross Value of Production

The gross value of production is the value of final products and marketable by-products available for sale or consumption on the farm. A high proportion of output on many semisubsistence farms is consumed by the home. If the value of goods consumed on the farm were excluded, output could be understated especially in many rural development projects designed to help the poorest farmers.

The value of intermediate goods produced on the farm is excluded when calculating the gross value of production to avoid double counting. Thus, if some of the grain produced on a farm is fed to livestock, the value of that portion of the grain output is not included in the gross value of production for the grain enterprise. It contributes to the livestock enterprise, and is accounted for automatically when the gross value of production for the livestock enterprise is calculated.

The gross value of production is calculated by multiplying the projected final output each year by the farm gate price, or the price at the point of first sale. It is usually incorrect to use the retail price to calculate the gross value of production, because the cost stream for agricultural production does not normally include the cost of marketing. If the project includes marketing the produce at some point outside the farm, however, project costs should include transport, marketing, and all other incidental costs. Similarly, if the project includes an element of processing, processing costs also should be included.

Inputs and outputs should be valued at constant prices. No allowance is made for price inflation, which is assumed to affect both costs and benefits equally. This assumption is obviously incorrect; but it is as obvious that the rate of inflation over the life of the project cannot be predicted accurately. To allow for inflation in estimating prices could create more errors than to assume constant prices. The analysis should reflect any likely real (relative) change in the price of any item, however. For example, benefits from agricultural or agro-industrial projects might accrue from an improvement in the quality of the product, or from a change in the time and the period of production or in the time of sale through processing, storage, or better handling. In such cases the prices of the products would be different with and without the project, and output should be valued at the appropriate price to reflect the changes. The same procedure would be applied where the effect of a large project is expected to reduce the price of output.

The gross value of production in project analysis is not always the same as the gross output of farm enterprises, which was discussed in Chapter 2. The gross output reflects the profitability of an enterprise or a farm on an annual basis. Adjustments are made, therefore, for opening and closing inventories, by considering the value of finished and unfinished goods (which would include, for instance, young steers not sold or consumed during the year). In the example given in Table 2–2, the gross output of cattle is obtained by subtracting the total of purchases and opening valuation from the total of sales and closing valuation of cattle. But in calculating the gross value of production for cattle, no adjustment would be made for the value of opening and closing inventories.

Loan Receipts and Grants

Loan receipts and grants boost inflows and reduce the amount that the farm family would need to contribute. The farm family's contribution of capital is not included in the inflows. It is reflected indirectly as the excess of outflows over inflows. Grants and loans may be in cash or in kind as the value of goods and services rendered. It is necessary to repay loans, but not grants. Repayment of loans is reflected under outflows as debt service.

Rental Value of the Farmhouse

The rental value of the farmhouse is the imputed value of the benefit the family derives from occupying the farmhouse. It is assessed at the normal market rate for comparable housing. Since the market for farmhouses in rural areas is usually inactive, it is difficult to arrive at a precise value. As a convenience, the annual rental value is sometimes assessed at from 5 to 10 percent of construction cost, depending on the kind of construction. It is necessary to assess rental value only when housing is included in the project costs. If the family owns a house without the project and is expected to live in it during the life of the project, rental value need not be assessed, because the value with the project would cancel out the value without the project. If credit is provided for house construction, the receipt of the loan would be shown as an inflow each year, the costs of construction as outflows, the rental value as inflows, and debt service as outflows. There would also be a salvage value for the house at the end of the project.

Salvage Value

Salvage value normally represents the residual market value or scrap value of assets used in the project. It might accrue at the end of the project or during the life of the project, if assets retaining marketable values are replaced from time to time. To obtain the salvage or residual value of an asset accruing from a project, it is sometimes necessary to calculate its incremental value. For example, if a cattle project expands or upgrades an existing herd that is productive without the project, the value of the herd without the project could not be ignored. That value would have to be subtracted from the salvage value of the herd at the end of the project to obtain the incremental salvage value arising from the project. In some projects with a long life or a high rate of return, the discounted salvage value of an asset is too small to have any significant influence on the internal rate of return.

Investment Costs

Investment costs for farm development cover expenditure for long-term development such as land clearing; drainage; irrigation; buildings; water supply; establishment of permanent crops; purchase of breeding stock, machinery, equipment; and the replacement costs for these items. Replacement costs are usually shown in those years when it is expected that assets would need to be replaced. Investment costs may be incurred directly by the farmer or indirectly by some agency on his behalf. In either case the financial analysis should show the total cost even though a portion might be offset by loans, grants, or subsidies. At the same time, the amounts of the loans, grants, or subsidies should be reflected under inflows. Since there is no difference in the result, some analysts prefer to show only the net expenditure. Showing the gross expenditure and the offsetting receipts separately, however, is helpful in preparing the economic analysis, because transfer payments, such as loans, grants, and subsidies, are not included in the economic analysis, but the gross expenditure is included.

Cash Operating Expenses

Cash operating expenses are those incurred for the day-to-day operation of the farm, and include the costs of hired labor paid in cash, fertilizer, seeds, sprays, materials, small tools, and transport. Processing and marketing costs are not included unless the project includes processing and marketing activities. Customs and excise duties, and sales, consumption, or other indirect taxes are also included; land taxes and income taxes are included where applicable. Normally the farmer buys goods at a market price, which already incorporates customs and excise duties, sales taxes, and other indirect taxes. Since the values of goods are normally recorded at market prices, no further adjustment is necessary in preparing the financial analysis. Social security payment, national insurance contributions, workmen's compensation, medical insurance, contributions to pension funds, and other payments made on behalf of labor employed on the farm are part of the labor cost and should be included in the financial analysis.

Subsidies and rebates, which reduce the farmer's cost, represent benefits to the farmer. If they are passed onto the farmer through a lower price for his inputs, no adjustment is necessary in the financial analysis. If, however, the farmer had to pay the full purchase price for an item and subsequently obtained a refund, the full cost would be shown as an outflow and the refund as an inflow under subsidies or grants.

Hired Labor Paid in Kind

In many communities, hired labor is compensated partly in cash and partly with produce from the farm. Payment by produce or other perquisites is referred to as payment in kind. Where produce is the medium of payment, the cost should be assessed by multiplying the quantity by the farm gate price of the commodity. Where some other method of payment is used, such as the right to use land, buildings, machinery, or animals, the value of the service rendered should be estimated and included as payment in kind. There are also other informal arrangements for the supply of labor, as mentioned in Chapter 5. In practice, however, a separate item for hired labor paid in kind might not show up in the financial analysis, because labor cost is usually projected on the basis of total labor requirements without any reference to the form of compensation. The entry for hired labor paid in kind merely draws attention to particular customs in the project area.

Debt Service

Debt service includes the payment of interest and the repayment of the loan principal. It may be calculated in different ways: as repayment of equal amounts of principal plus interest on the diminishing balance after each installment, or as level payment (equated annuity), assuming no grace period. Interest during the grace period may be paid when it is due, or may be added to the principal to be repaid as part of the total amount due by level payment during the repayment period. [2] Some other ways of calculating debt service may be used, depending on the cash flow position of the farm.

"Credit is often a key element in the modernization of agriculture. Not only can it remove a financial constraint, but it may provide the incentive to adopt new technologies that would be more slowly accepted." [3] To be effective, credit should be easily accessible, in the right amount, in the right place, at the right time, with maximum flexibility for repayment, and with minimum bureaucratic intervention. Debt service policies have serious implications for the credit institution as well as for the farmer. Credit terms should be attractive enough to motivate the farmer to achieve a higher level of performance, but stringent enough to protect the viability of the lending institution. Large loans with little or no down payment, a generous grace period, long maturities, and low interest rates might be a windfall to the farmers who manage to get them. But for the credit institution with limited resources, such loans have a slow rate of recovery and would reduce its ability to provide similar facilities to other farmers in the future. Moreover, credit institutions that charge rates of interest that are too low to cover the operating cost cannot survive without being subsidized at the expense of other sectors of the economy. Thus, credit should be profitable to the farmer as well as to the lending institution.

Farm Family Net Benefit

The farm family net benefit is the difference between inflows and outflows. It represents the amount that the farm family has to live on after paying

2. See J. Price Gittinger, "Agricultural Loan Repayment Computation Review Exercise," EDI course material, AE–1024–P&S (Washington, D.C.: World Bank, 1973; processed), which discusses these methods and provides problem and solution sets.

3. World Bank, "Bank Policy on Agricultural Credit," 436 (a restricted-circulation document) (Washington, D.C., 1974; processed).

all business expenses and debt service, if participation in the project is the family's only source of income. It is not unusual for the farm family net benefit to be negative in the early life of the project, especially with projects that have a long gestation period. The amount of the negative farm family net benefit represents the capital that the farm family must contribute from its own resources. Questions often arise as to whether farmers will be attracted to projects with a negative farm family net benefit stream at the beginning of the project. Participation, however, is often related to expectation of profitability,[4] which is not measured by the farm family net benefit flow. In addition, although bigger loans on softer terms may result in more attractive farm family net benefit flows, fewer farms will benefit from the project under the constraint of limited resources.

Farm Family Net Benefit without the Project

In project analysis, the value of previously owned land, existing capital, labor, and management contributed by the farm family are not shown as explicit costs among the project outflows. They are reflected at their opportunity cost, and their combined value is represented by the farm family net benefit without the project. This is obtained by subtracting the outflows without the project from the inflows without the project (see Table 7–1).

As an example, suppose that a family must shift from the production of short-term crops to that of permanent tree crops to participate in a project. The family, then, would have to give up the income (or farm family net benefit) it previously derived from producing short-term crops. This is the opportunity cost of making the change. In preparing a financial analysis for the project, the outflows would not include the costs of land, family labor, management, and existing capital. These are valued at their opportunity cost, which is represented by the farm family net benefit that would have been derived from producing short-term crops without the project.

This principle is fairly simple to apply where the farm family is occupied full-time on the farm without the project. But it is not unusual for the farm family to have some part-time outside employment to supplement farm income. If participation in a project entails giving up such employment, the income foregone is a true cost to the project and should be added to the inflows without the project. Thus, the additional input of

---

4. Annual profitability is ascertained by calculating the net farm income, as discussed in Chapter 2.

family labor on the farm necessitated by the project would be reflected in the farm family net benefit without the project. For example, the opportunity cost for a teacher considering a shift to full-time farming in order to participate in the project is the income he gives up to farm full-time. Thus, in preparing the financial analysis, the farm family net benefit without the project would be the projected annual salary which he would earn as a teacher. If the decision to participate in the project is based purely on monetary considerations, the farm family net benefit with the project would have to be great enough to compensate him not only for the capital invested in the project, but also for the salary he has to give up to become a full-time farmer.

In a stable farming situation it is not unlikely that the farm family net benefit without the project would have remained constant as shown in Table 7–2. Situations do exist, however, where farm family net benefit could be expected to decrease progressively if the project were not implemented, for example, in a case of declining soil fertility due to poor drainage. It is also possible that even without the project being implemented, productivity could be expected to increase because of previous improvements in the designated project area. In such circumstances where it is not expected that the farm family net benefit would remain constant over the life of the project, a corresponding table should be prepared to show what the inflows, outflows, and farm family net benefit would be without the project. A single column for the without project situation as shown in Table 7–1 and in 7–2 (below) would not be adequate.

Incremental Farm Family Net Benefit

The incremental farm family net benefit is obtained by subtracting the farm family net benefit without the project from the farm family net benefit with the project. This accounts automatically for the cost of the farm family's contribution of owned land, labor, management, and existing capital. The remaining incremental farm family net benefit thus represents only the return on the new capital invested in the project by the farm family.

Financial Rate of Return after Financing

The financial rate of return after financing represents the rate of return on capital contributed by the farm family. In calculating this rate, loans and debt service charges are included in the analysis.

Table 7-2. *Financial Analysis, after Financing, for the Egg Production Model* (thousands of pesos)

Item	Without project	With project (years)				
		1	2	3-8[a]	9	10
(a) Inflows						
Gross value of production	153.19	154.23	312.29	459.58	459.58	459.58
Loan receipts (90 percent of investment)	...	91.96	67.63	...	...	...
Salvage value (incremental)		...	...	...	...	22.53
Total	153.19	246.19	379.92	459.58	459.58	482.11
(b) Outflows						
Investment costs	...	102.18	75.14	...	...	...
Cash operating expenses	123.49	123.49	230.96	372.33	372.33	372.33
Debt service	...	5.52	15.10	38.82	...	...
Total	123.49	231.19	321.20	411.15	372.33	372.33
(c) Farm family net benefit (a − b)	29.70	15.00	58.72	48.43	87.25	109.78
(d) Farm family net benefit without project[b]	29.70	29.70	29.70	29.70	29.70	29.70
(e) Incremental farm family net benefit (cash flow) (c − d)	...	−14.70	29.02	18.73	57.55	80.08

Financial rate of return on the farm family's capital = more than 50 percent

... Zero or negligible.
a. For each year of the period.
b. From the first column for item c.
Source: Adapted from World Bank, "Appraisal of the Second Livestock Project—Philippines."

Generally the incremental farm family net benefit is negative in the early life of the project and is positive in the later years. The discount rate that equalizes the total present worths of the negative and positive values in the incremental farm family net benefit stream is referred to as the internal financial rate of return. It is called an internal rate of return because it is generated within the project by the iterative process of discounting the incremental farm family net benefit stream.

Table 7–2 illustrates the steps in calculating the financial rate of return on the farm family's capital for the egg production model discussed in Chapter 6. The basic data for the analysis are given in Table 7–3, the gross value of production and cash operating expenses, and Table 7–4, investment costs.

In this model, the financial rate of return on the capital invested by the farm family is greater than 50 percent. This result is attributable to the following factors: (a) the output/input price relation is favorable; (b) capital is not tied up for a long time in building up assets; (c) substantial benefits begin to flow early in the life of the project; (d) debt servicing is not onerous; and (e) 90 percent of the investment is financed by a soft loan.

Projects with these characteristics generally have a high rate of return (though not necessarily as high as 50 percent), because the cash flow becomes positive quite early in the life of the project. Broiler and egg production, fattening operations for livestock, and production of short-term crops usually belong to this category. But there is no general rule. A change in one or more of the favorable factors could give the opposite result unless compensated for by other factors. Projects with a negative cash flow for a long period would have less attractive rates of return unless other conditions, such as the output/input price relation, manage to offset the effect of the long maturation period. Examples of such projects are those which involve the production of permanent tree crops, forestry, and livestock breeding.

Table 7–5 presents the financial analysis after financing for the cattle breeding/fattening project to be introduced on a twenty hectare coconut plantation. The terms of the loan are similar to those in the egg production project. Ninety percent of the investment is covered by loans to be repaid in ten years, including a four year grace period. The rate of interest is 12 percent. The herd buildup in this project was given earlier in Table 6–11. Table 7–6 gives the gross value of production and cash operating expenses, and Table 7–7 shows the investment costs for the project.

The financial rate of return on the farm family's capital for this project is 19 percent, as shown in Table 7–5. During the first ten years of the project the incremental farm family net benefit is positive only in the fourth year. In other words, in nine of these years, the farm family would

Table 7–3. *Gross Value of Production and Cash Operating Expenses for the Egg Production Model*

Item (unit)	Price/ unit (pesos)	Without project		With project (year) 1		2		3–10	
		Number of units	Amount (thousands of pesos)	Number of units	Amount (thousands of pesos)	Number of units	Amount (thousands of pesos)	Number of units	Amount (thousands of pesos)
Gross value of production									
Eggs (number)	0.38	372,300	141.47	372,300	141.47	773,727	294.02	1,116,900	424.42
Culled hens (number)	7.00	934	6.54	934	6.54	934	6.54	2,800	19.60
Droppings (kilograms)	0.10	21,250	2.12	25,500	2.55	48,070	4.81	63,750	6.38
Feed bags (number)	2.00	1,530	3.06	1,836	3.67	3,461	6.92	4,590	9.18
Total			153.19		154.23		312.29		459.58
Cash operating expenses									
Day-old chicks (number)	2.70	1,500	4.05	1,500	4.05	1,500	4.05	4,500	12.15
Feed									
Starter/grower (kilograms)	1.28	16,992	21.75	16,992	21.75	16,992	21.75	51,000	65.28
Layer (kilograms)	1.32	68,000	89.76	68,000	89.76	141,320	186.54	204,000	269.28
Medicines, vaccines, and supplements	—	—	2.23	—	2.23	—	4.17	—	6.69
Electricity and water	—	—	1.12	—	1.12	—	2.08	—	3.35
Labor	—	—	1.08	—	1.08	—	2.16	—	3.24
Repairs and miscellaneous	—	—	3.50	—	3.50	—	10.21	—	12.34
Total			123.49		123.49		230.96		372.33

— Not applicable.
Source: Same as for Table 7–2.

102

Table 7-4. *Investment Costs for the Egg Production Model*

Item (unit)	Size of unit	Unit cost (pesos)	Year 1		Year 2		Total	
			Number of units	Cost (pesos)	Number of units	Cost (pesos)	Number of units	Cost (pesos)
Fixed								
Brooder/grower (square meters)	77.50	172[a]	1	13,330	...	...	1	13,330
Laying house (square meters)	86.16	223[a]	2	38,428	1	19,214	3	57,642
Store room (square meters)	11.52	200[a]	2	4,608	1	2,304	3	6,912
Workers quarters (square meters)	20.00	300[a]	1	6,000	—	—	1	6,912
Water system	—	—	1	10,000	—	—	1	6,000
Miscellaneous	—	—	1	2,000	—	—	1	10,000
							—	2,000
Subtotal				74,366		21,518		95,884
Incremental working capital								
Chick purchase	—	2.70	1,500	4,050	3,000	8,100	4,500	12,150
Feed (kilograms)	—	1.28[b]	16,992	21,750	33,984	43,500	50,976	65,250
Medicines, vaccines, and supplements	—	—	—	435	—	870	—	1,305
Electricity and water	—	—	—	218	—	435	—	653
Labor	—	—	—	359	—	718	—	1,077
Miscellaneous	—	—	—	1,000	—	—	—	1,000
Subtotal				27,812		53,623		81,435
Total investment				102,178		75,141		177,319

— Not applicable.
a. Per square meter.
b. Per kilogram.
Source: Same as for Table 7-2.

103

Table 7–5. *Financial Analysis, after Financing, for the Integrated Coconut and Cattle Breeding and Fattening Model*
(thousands of pesos)

Item	Without project	With project (year)					
		1	2	3	4	5	6
(a) Inflows							
Gross value of production	19.00	19.00	22.80	31.08	53.12	59.14	58.34
Loan receipts (90 percent of investment)	...	44.29	44.46	19.34	...	...	...
Salvage value (incremental)	...	...	...	...	...	...	...
Total	19.00	63.29	67.26	50.42	53.12	59.14	58.34
(b) Outflows							
Investment costs	...	49.22	49.40	21.49	...	...	...
Cash operating expenses	4.43	4.43	5.94	6.76	21.25	25.53	23.55
Debt service	...	2.66	7.98	11.81	12.97	26.29	26.29
Total	4.43	56.31	63.32	40.06	34.22	51.82	49.84
(c) Farm family net benefit (a − b)	14.57	6.98	3.94	10.36	18.90	7.32	8.50
(d) Farm family net benefit without project	14.57	14.57	14.57	14.57	14.57	14.57	14.57
(e) Incremental farm family net benefit (cash flow) (c − d)	...	−7.59	−10.63	−4.21	4.33	−7.25	−6.07

Table 7-5 (continued)

Item	With project (year)					
	7–9	10	11–14	15	16–19	20
(a) Inflows						
Gross value of production	62.72	64.22	62.72	64.22	62.72	62.72
Loan receipts (90 percent of investment)	...	...	...	...	...	
Salvage value (incremental)	...	...	...	...	...	55.26
Total	62.72	64.22	62.72	64.22	62.72	117.98
(b) Outflows						
Investment costs	...	...	...	...	...	...
Cash operating expenses	23.55	26.70	23.55	26.70	23.55	23.55
Debt service	26.69	26.69	...	...	...	...
Total	49.84	52.99	23.55	26.70	23.55	23.55
(c) Farm family net benefit (a − b)	12.88	11.23	39.17	37.52	39.17	94.41
(d) Farm family net benefit without project	14.57	14.57	14.57	14.57	14.57	14.57
(e) Incremental farm family net benefit (cash flow) (c − d)	−1.69	−3.34	24.60	22.95	24.60	79.84

Financial rate of return on the farm family's capital = 19 percent

... Zero or negligible.
Source: Same as for Table 7–2.

105

Table 7-6. Gross Value of Production and Cash Operating Expenses for the Integrated Coconut and Cattle Breeding and Fattening Model (thousands of pesos)

Item	Without project	With project (year)					
		1	2	3	4	5	6
Gross value of production							
Copra	19.00	19.00	22.80	26.80	31.22	34.96	38.47
Cattle							
Cull bull	...	...	...	...	...	1.50	...
Cull cows	...	...	...	2.40	3.60	3.60	3.60
Weaners	...	...	...	...	3.90	4.68	5.46
Steers, 1–2 years	...	...	...	2.00	...	...	...
Steers, 2–3 years	...	...	...	...	14.40	14.40	10.80
Total sales	19.00	19.00	22.80	31.08	53.12	59.14	58.33
Cash operating expenses							
Labor							
Copra making	3.80	3.80	4.56	5.34	6.64	6.99	7.69
Cowboy	...	...	...	...	1.36	1.71	2.08
Animal health	...	...	...	...	0.78	0.76	0.80
Bull replacement	...	...	...	...	...	3.00	...
Repairs and maintenance	0.42	0.42	1.08	1.10	1.10	1.10	1.10
Fertilizer							
Pastures	...	...	...	...	2.20	2.20	2.20
Coconuts	...	...	...	...	8.55	8.55	8.55
Miscellaneous (5 percent)	0.21	0.21	0.28	0.32	1.01	1.22	1.12
Total operating expenses	4.43	4.43	5.92	6.76	21.64	25.53	23.54

Table 7-6 (continued)

Item	With project (year)					
	7	8–9	10	11–14	15	16–20
Gross value of production						
Copra	38.47	38.47	38.47	38.47	38.47	38.47
Cattle						
Cull bull	...	...	...	...	...	...
Cull cows	...	...	1.50	...	1.50	...
Weaners	3.60	3.60	3.60	3.60	3.60	3.60
Steers, 1–2 years	6.24	6.24	6.24	6.24	6.24	6.24
Steers, 2–3 years	14.40	14.40	14.40	14.40	14.40	14.40
Total sales	62.71	62.71	64.21	62.71	64.21	62.71
Cash operating expenses						
Labor						
Copra making	7.69	7.69	7.69	7.69	7.69	7.69
Cowboy	2.08	2.08	2.08	2.08	2.08	2.08
Animal health	0.80	0.80	0.80	0.80	0.80	0.80
Bull replacement			3.00		3.00	
Repairs and maintenance	1.10	1.10	1.10	1.10	1.10	1.10
Fertilizer						
Pastures	2.20	2.20	2.20	2.20	2.20	2.20
Coconuts	8.55	8.55	8.55	8.55	8.55	8.55
Miscellaneous (5 percent)	1.12	1.12	1.12	1.12	1.12	1.12
Total operating expenses	23.54	23.54	26.69	23.54	26.69	23.54

... Zero or negligible.
Source: Same as for Table 7–2.

Table 7-7. Investment Costs for the Integrated Coconut and Cattle Breeding and Fattening Model

Investment item (unit)	Unit cost (pesos)	Year 1		Year 2		Year 3		Total	
		Number of units	Cost (pesos)	Number of units	Cost (pesos)	Number of units	Cost (pesos)	Number of units	Cost (pesos)
Fixed									
Grass and legume pasture (hectares)	760	10	7,600	10	7,600	...	...	20	15,200
Fencing (kilometers)	3,710	2.5	9,275	...	...	...	...	2.5	9,275
Water system (number)	2,000	1	2,000	...	...	...	...	1	2,000
Improved copra drier (number)	400	1	400	...	...	...	...	1	400
Corral (number)	2,000	1	2,000	...	...	...	...	1	2,000
Bulls (number)	3,000	1	3,000	...	...	...	...	1	3,000
Heifers, 1–2 years (number)	1,500	9	13,500	19	28,500	...	...	28	42,000
Miscellaneous (5 percent)	...	...	1,890	...	1,805	...	...	...	3,695
Subtotal	...	...	39,665	...	77,570	...	...	...	...
Incremental working capital									
Feeder steers, 1–2 years (number)	1,000	...	...	...	...	8	8,000	8	8,000
Animal health (animal units)	20	10	200	29	580	37	740	76	1,520
Cowboy's salary (man-weeks)	40	9	360	18	720	25	1,000	52	2,080
Fertilizer									
Pastures (sacks)	110	...	...	10	1,100	20	2,200	30	3,300
Coconuts (sacks)	95	90	8,550	90	8,550	90	8,550	270	25,650
Miscellaneous (5 percent)	...	...	450	...	540	...	997	...	1,987
Subtotal	...	...	9,560	...	11,490	...	21,487	...	42,537
Total investment	...	...	49,225	...	49,225	...	21,487	...	120,107

... Zero or negligible.
Source: Same as for Table 7–2.

108

Table 7-8. *Analysis, before Financing, for the Egg Production Model*
(thousands of pesos)

Item	Without project	With project (year) 1	2	3-9[a]	10
(a) Inflows					
Gross value of production	153.19	154.23	312.29	459.58	459.58
Salvage value (incremental)	...	...	...	...	22.53
Total	153.19	154.23	312.29	459.58	482.11
(b) Outflows					
Investment costs	...	102.18	75.14	...	...
Cash operating expenses	123.49	123.49	230.96	372.33	372.33
Total	123.49	225.67	306.10	372.33	372.33
(c) Farm family net benefit (a − b)	29.70	−71.44	6.19	87.25	109.78
(d) Farm family net benefit without project[b]	29.70	29.70	29.70	29.70	29.70
(e) Incremental farm family net benefit (cash flow) (c − d)	...	−101.14	−23.51	57.55	80.08
Financial rate of return on the total investment = 33 percent					

... Zero or negligible.
a. For each year of the period.
b. From the first column for item c.
Source: Same as for Table 7-2.

Table 7-9. Financial Analysis, before and after Financing, for the Egg Production Model
(thousands of pesos)

Item	Without project	With project (year)				
		1	2	3–8ᵃ	9	10
(a) Inflows						
Gross value of production	153.19	154.23	312.29	459.58	459.58	459.58
Salvage value (incremental)	...	...	...	...	...	22.53
Total	153.19	154.23	312.29	459.58	459.58	482.11
(b) Outflows						
Investment costs	...	102.18	75.14	...	...	...
Cash operating expenses	123.49	123.49	230.96	372.33	372.33	372.33
Total	123.49	225.67	306.10	372.33	372.33	372.33
(c) Farm family net benefit (a − b)	29.70	−71.44	6.19	87.25	87.25	109.78
(d) Farm family net benefit without project	29.70	29.70	29.70	29.70	29.70	29.70
(e) Incremental farm family net benefit (before financing) (cash flow) (c − d)	...	−101.14	−23.51	57.55	57.55	80.08
Financial rate of return on the total investment = 33 percent						
(f) Financing						
Loans		91.96	67.63	...	...	...
Debt service		5.52	15.10	38.82	...	...
Net financing		86.44	52.53	−38.82	...	...
(g) Incremental farm family net benefit (after financing)		−14.70	29.02	18.73	57.55	80.08
Financial rate of return on the farm family's capital = > 50 percent						

... Zero or negligible.
a. For each year of the period.
b. From the first column for item c.
Source: Same as for Table 7-2.

have less to live on with the project than without the project. Although the value of the herd is growing during this time, this does not benefit the cash position of the family. This is one reason why cattle breeding projects, or other projects with a long gestation period, often prove unattractive to small farmers who do not have a supplementary source of financing or substantial income outside the farm to enable them to survive until the project can support them.

Financial Rate of Return before Financing

One reason given for the high financial rate of return in the egg production project presented in Table 7–2 is that 90 percent of the investment is financed by a soft loan. Thus, the cash flow position is very favorable in the early life of the project. In fact year 1 is the only year in which the incremental farm family net benefit is negative. In general, any increase in the percentage of investment cost financed by sources outside the farm will push up the financial rate of return on the capital contributed by the farm family.

But this rate, which is influenced by the terms of financing, is not a true indication of profitability over the life of a project. To test the intrinsic profitability of a project, loan receipts and debt service should be excluded from the financial analysis. The financial rate of return calculated on this basis reflects the return on the total investment, not merely the farm family's contribution. As shown in Table 7–8, the financial rate of return on the total investment for the egg production model falls to 33 percent.

The financial analysis before and after financing can be incorporated in a single table, by listing financing costs in a separate category, as illustrated in Table 7–9.

It is sometimes felt that the financial analysis before financing can be used as a basis to calculate credit needs. The inflows sometime include noncash items, however, such as the rental value of the farmhouse, or the value of produce consumed in the home (which is included in the gross value of production). To calculate the credit needs of the project, adjustment should be made for all noncash elements of costs and benefits that may be included in the accounts. A somewhat better approach is to prepare a separate budget for financial resources, as illustrated in Tables 5–8 and 5–9. Then the credit needs of the project can be reflected, as desired, on a monthly, quarterly, or seasonal basis.

8

•-●-•

Economic Analysis

The economic analysis of a project reflects its profitability from the viewpoint of society as a whole. Profitability in this context is defined as the capacity of the project to maximize the efficient use of a nation's resources in producing national income. This capacity can be measured in any of the three discounted measures of project worth outlined in Chapter 4: the benefit/cost ratio, the net present worth, and the economic rate of return. As mentioned before, the economic rate of return has certain advantages over the benefit/cost ratio and the net present worth, and it is the measure most commonly used by the World Bank and many other international organizations as one of the criteria for selecting projects for financing. This chapter begins, therefore, by outlining the procedures for calculating the economic rate of return. The format of the analysis, however, can also facilitate the calculation of the benefit/cost ratio and the net present worth.

Despite the importance of the economic analysis, economic efficiency is not the sole criterion for selecting projects to implement. Stronger influences are sometimes exerted by other factors such as political considerations, the capacity of a project to provide employment and to distribute income, regional development, environmental protection, and defense. These criteria do not invalidate the importance of the economic analysis, however, since it provides more than just calculations of the economic rate of return, the benefit/cost ratio, or the net present worth. Preparing the economic analysis provides a framework within which the various relations inherent in the project can be tested in a systematic way; poor projects can be recognized easily; questionable assumptions can be brought to light; and inconsistencies can be resolved. Economic analysis also provides the basis for the systematic reshaping of projects; poorly designed projects can be upgraded, and good projects can be made better.

Several systems have been advocated for preparing the economic analysis. The most important ones include: (a) the OECD (Office of Economic Cooperation and Development) method proposed by Little and Mirrlees,[1] (b) the UNIDO (United Nations Industrial Development Organization) method proposed by Dasgupta, Marglin, and Sen,[2] (c) the Squire/van der Tak approach,[3] and (d) the traditional method used by the World Bank.[4] The four approaches lead to basically the same results in practice. The most important differences are in the definition of the numéraire, or unit of account.[5] The OECD method uses untied foreign exchange available for use by the government as the numéraire. Squire and van der Tak define a similar numéraire. The UNIDO method proposes aggregate consumption; whereas the traditional World Bank method uses national income. The differences in the numéraire are basically variations which have the same objectives and which lead in most cases to the same results. This discussion is based on the more traditional method used by the World Bank, which usually involves less calculation in analyzing agricultural projects.

The economic analysis, which can be prepared from data used for the financial analysis, differs from the latter in two important respects. First, the economic analysis is concerned with flows of real resources. Second, in the economic analysis, resources are valued in terms of their opportunity cost, which may be different from their market prices. Therefore, in the transition from the financial analysis to the economic analysis, adjustments must be made to exclude transfer payments, loan receipts, and debt service, and to remove distortions in the prices of foreign exchange, inputs, and outputs.

Adjusting Transfer Payments

Transfer payments involve flows of income between the government and the people in the society. Transfers from the people to the government

1. See I. M. D. Little and J. A. Mirrles, *Project Appraisal and Planning for the Developing Countries* (London: Heineminn Educational Books, 1974), which is a revised version of *Manual of Industrial Project Analysis* (Paris: Organization for Economic Cooperation and Development, 1969).
2. United Nations Industrial Development Organization, *Guidelines for Project Evaluation* (New York: United Nations, 1972).
3. Lyn Squire and Herman G. van der Tak, *Economic Analysis of Projects* (Baltimore: Johns Hopkins University Press, 1975).
4. J. Price Gittinger, *Economic Analysis of Agricultural Projects* (Baltimore: Johns Hopkins University Press, 1972).
5. Eugene R. Schlesinger, "The Use of Numeraires in Social Cost-Benefit Analysis: An Introductory Overview", EDI Course Material, CN–841 (Washington, D.C.: World Bank, 1978; processed).

include customs duties, excise duties, tariffs, land and corporation taxes, sales taxes, other indirect taxes, social security payments, and contributions to pension funds. Transfers from the government to the people include subsidies and grants.

Transfer payments may be shown as separate items of benefits and costs or may be incorporated in prices used in the financial analysis. If they can be identified, they should be excluded when preparing the economic analysis. If they are incorporated in other items, they should be systematically traced and appropriately adjusted so that their effect in the financial analysis would not be carried over into the economic analysis.

Loans and debt service can be regarded as transfer payments between borrowers and lenders. Loans and debt service do not actually "use up" real resources and therefore should not be included in the economic analysis.

Adjusting the Price of Foreign Exchange

The foreign exchange rate expresses the number of units of the local currency that can be exchanged for one unit of the currency of some other country. For example, when the exchange rate is Rs 10 = $1.00, this means that ten rupees is the price of one dollar, the unit of foreign currency. The foreign exchange rate therefore provides the basis for settling transactions between one country and another.

In project analysis, the official exchange rate (OER) is distinguished from the shadow exchange rate (SER). The OER is the rate established by the central government or the central bank of a country as the basis for facilitating international transactions. It is the rate used to value imports and exports in preparing the financial analysis. Quite often, however, this rate is either overvalued or undervalued because of imbalances and distortions within the structure of the economy. If the OER of, say, Rs10 = $1.00 happens to be overvalued, it means that one dollar of foreign exchange will buy imported goods which are worth more than ten rupees in the domestic market, given the trade and foreign exchange policies of the government; or, alternatively, that it would require more than ten rupees of local resources to produce goods which could be exported for one dollar or which could substitute for one dollar's worth of imports. Using an overvalued or undervalued OER reflects improper relations between the prices of domestic and foreign resources and seriously distorts the allocation of resources.

Whenever the OER is considered to be inappropriate, the SER or some other adjustment must be introduced to give a more reliable estimate of the purchasing power of foreign exchange. This will not remove the distortions in the economic system, but it will lead to greater economic efficiency in allocating resources.

Distortions in the pricing of foreign exchange can arise from natural and artificial barriers to trade. Natural barriers are those inherent in the goods involved, such as its value in relation to its bulk and weight, distance from the foreign market, freight and shipping charges, and insurance. These factors help to determine the comparative advantage a country has in supplying the goods. Artificial barriers are those imposed by the government to encourage exports and to discourage imports through subsidies on exports, tariffs on imports, quotas, licensing, bans, foreign exchange restrictions, and other regulations. These artificial barriers create or maintain a divergence between the OER and the real purchasing power of the domestic currency.

The extent of the distortion in the local currency needs to be estimated to calculate the SER. This requires special skills and an intimate knowledge of the foreign exchange situation in a country. One simple recommendation is to "use the shadow price (that is, the rate of exchange) that the central planning unit is using."[6] This approach is justified by the fact that "if some projects use one shadow price for foreign exchange and others use another, the whole point of using shadow prices to value import content correctly and uniformly is lost."[7] Of course if the planning unit is unable or unwilling to suggest the appropriate SER, the analyst has to calculate an acceptable rate based on some weighted average of the premium for foreign exchange in the formal market and the black market.

Adjusting the Price of Inputs

Inputs may be divided into four categories: the nonproduced inputs (land and labor); locally produced inputs; imported inputs; and mixed-component inputs. Since each category of input is valued differently, the farm budgets should specify the quantity and value of each category of input so that prices may be adjusted for the economic analysis.

Nonproduced inputs

The principles governing the economic valuation of land and labor were discussed in Chapter 5. For both inputs the main criterion is the oppor-

6. Gittinger, *Economic Analysis of Agricultural Projects*, p. 39.
7. Ibid.

tunity cost. The rules for valuing land and labor are summarized in that chapter.

Locally produced inputs

The valuation of locally produced inputs depends on whether they would normally be exported if there was no project, and, if not, whether there is excess capacity in the producing industry to serve the project demand. The simple guidelines for calculating the opportunity cost for the alternative uses of locally produced inputs is as follows:

Alternative uses	*Opportunity cost*
Item is exported (diverted exports).	Foreign exchange losses (f.o.b.) at SER.[8]
Item is not exported, and there is no excess capacity in the producing industry (diverted domestic use).	Price paid by alternative user (that is, market price), adjusted for transfer payments.
Sufficient excess capacity exists to fulfill project demand (expanded production).	Cost of variable resources used up in producing item for project (that is, the variable costs).

Imported inputs

Inputs that are obtained from foreign sources are usually quoted in the currency of the supplying country and are converted into the currency of the importing country by multiplying the c.i.f. (cost, insurance, freight) value by the OER. This gives the border price used in financial analysis. But the currency of most developing countries is often overvalued, and the OER does not always reflect the opportunity cost of the foreign currency. It is therefore necessary to adjust the border price by the premium on foreign exchange. Alternatively, the economic value of the input can be calculated by multiplying its c.i.f. value expressed in foreign currency by the SER.[9]

Incidental costs of importation (such as port charges and local transport and marketing costs) included in the financial analysis should also be

8. The loss of foreign exchange is estimated by calculating the export parity, as illustrated in Table 8–1. Export parity is discussed in William A. Ward, "Calculating Import and Export Parity Prices," EDI course material, CN–3 (Washington, D.C.: World Bank, 1976; processed).
9. For the calculation of the shadow exchange rate, see William A. Ward, "Adjusting for Over-Valued Domestic Currency: Shadow Exchange Rates and Conversion Factors," EDI Course Material, CN–28 (Washington, D.C.: World Bank, 1976; processed).

reflected in the economic analysis, but tariffs and subsidies should be excluded, as should all other transfer payments.

Governments frequently adopt protectionist policies, which prohibit or restrict the importation of certain inputs, although the supply of these items from domestic sources may be inadequate or may be of inferior quality. These restrictions usually raise the market price for the preferred imported item. If a project is designed to use the imported item, using the import parity price (which might be lower than the domestic price) would underestimate the economic value of the item. The higher domestic price of the imported item should be used to value the input, as it more accurately reflects the opportunity cost of the item. It represents what other potential users are willing to pay, based on the value of the benefit from the best alternative use they would forego, if the imported item were diverted to the project. If, however, the project is designed to use the less preferred domestic item, the opportunity cost to be used in the economic analysis would be the import parity price for the less preferred domestic item, and the production of output would be related to the efficiency of the locally produced item.

Mixed-component inputs

Mixed-component inputs are those which are supplied locally, but which contain a portion of the cost attributable to imported raw materials. To obtain the proper value for the economic analysis, the financial cost must be broken down into its foreign and domestic components, and the proper rules must be applied for the economic valuation of each part, as discussed earlier.

Adjusting the Price of Outputs

Project outputs may be conveniently divided into five major categories: (a) exports; (b) import substitutes; (c) locally consumed output that would not have been supplied without the project; (d) intermediate products; and (e) intangible benefits. Most projects contain elements of more than one of these categories. As different valuation systems are used for each category of output, the farm budgets should specify the quantity and value of each category of output so that prices may be adjusted for the economic analysis.

Exported outputs

The economic value of exported output is measured by its foreign exchange earnings. This is calculated by deducting insurance and freight charges from the c.i.f. value of output landed in the importing country. This gives the border price expressed in foreign currency. The local currency equivalent, which is also called the export parity price, is obtained by multiplying the border price by the SER.[10] Project costs for exported goods normally include marketing, transport, and handling charges; if these costs are not included, they should be deducted from the local currency equivalent. Table 8–1 shows the steps to calculate the export parity price.

Table 8–1. *Calculating Export Parity Price*

Financial analysis
　c.i.f. at port of entry
　　minus　Freight
　　minus　Insurance
　　minus　Unloading at port of entry
　　equals　f.o.b. at port of entry
　　convert　Foreign currency to domestic currency at OER
　　minus　Tariffs
　　plus　Subsidies
　　minus　Local port charges
　　minus　Local costs of storage, loading, and inland transport and marketing
　　　　　costs, only if they are not part of project costs
　　equals　Export parity price

Economic analysis
　f.o.b. at port
　　convert　Foreign currency to domestic at SER
　　minus　Local costs of storage, loading, and inland transport marketing costs,
　　　　　only if they are not part of project costs
　　equals　Economic value of export

Source: Ward, "Calculating Import and Export Parity Prices," p. 8.

Governments sometimes adopt policies to restrict or prohibit the export of certain goods which are usually exported in order to encourage low consumer prices on the domestic market. If, during project preparation, certain items produced by the project are not expected to be exported during the life of the project, the economic value of such goods should not be measured by the export parity price. Their value should be based on the farm gate price or the price at the point of first sale, either of which might be lower than the export parity price. This lower price more accurately reflects the value of such goods to society.

10. Ward, "Calculating Import and Export Parity Prices."

Import substitutes

An import substitute is a good produced locally to replace a similar or comparable good that would otherwise be imported. The economic value of an import substitute is measured by the saving in foreign exchange. This is calculated by multiplying the c.i.f. value of the item by the SER to obtain the border price expressed in local currency. This is also referred to as the import parity price [11] or the import substitution value. The import parity price must be adjusted by adding transport costs and other associated changes for handling and storage between the port and the market, and by subtracting those from the market to the project to obtain the value of the output at the project site. In the absence of protection, the maximum price for which the good can be sold in the market is the landed cost plus transport and other associated charges. Therefore the maximum price that can be charged at the project site would be the market price minus the cost of transport and other associated charges from the project to the market.

Whenever the imported item and the import substitute differ in quality, the import parity price must be adjusted. If the import substitute is more highly regarded than the imported item, the import parity price will set the lower limit for the economic valuation; if the imported item is considered more valuable, the import parity price sets the upper limit.

A distinction should be made between calculating the import parity price for a processed good and for the raw material from which it is derived. Projects may produce only raw material, only processed goods from purchased raw material, or both. When the project incorporates the processing stage, the import parity price for the processed good should be calculated. When the project involves only the production of raw material, however, the import parity price for the raw material should be calculated, which includes adjustment for processing costs and the conversion ratio for raw material into final product.

Table 8–2 illustrates the calculation of the import parity price for paddy produced in Gambia as a substitute for rice imported from Burma. The World Bank's forecast for rice of a similar grade was US$81.45 a ton f.o.b. (free on board) Rangoon. The SER was assumed to be equal to the OER of D1.92 = US$1. The milling output of rice to paddy was 66 percent. The import parity price of paddy at the farm gate was found to be D118 a ton.

11. Ibid.

Table 8–2. *Import Parity Price of Paddy*
(per ton)

Value of milled rice		
Milled rice f.o.b. Rangoon		US$81.45
plus	Freight to the Gambia	22.88
plus	Insurance	0.28
plus	Harbor dues	0.78
plus	Fumigation	0.52
plus	Handling and so forth	1.56
Milled rice c.i.f. Gambia		US$107.47
Converting (OER of D1.92 = US$1)		D206.34
plus	Storage costs in Gambia	10.82
Wholesale cost of imported rice		D217.16
Value of paddy		
Value of 1-ton paddy at conversion rate		
of 66 percent		= D143.32
minus	Milling cost	D13.00
minus	Transport	3.85
minus	Storage	8.63
		25.48
Import parity price for 1 ton of paddy		D117.84

Source: World Bank, "Appraisal for an Agricultural Development Project—The Gambia," PA–142a (a restricted-circulation document) (Washington, D.C., August 8, 1972; processed), Annex 7, Table 1.

Locally consumed outputs

Locally consumed outputs are goods that would not have been supplied by imports without the project. [12] This category includes goods sold off the farm and those consumed on the farm. The general rule for valuing these items is to use the farm gate price, or the price at the point of first sale after deducting subsidies and other transfer payments. Crop bonuses, premiums, and other incentives paid as part of the purchase price to achieve quantitative or qualitative production targets are included in the price, because they represent payment for real resources rather than mere transfer payments.

Intermediate products

In agricultural project analysis, final products are distinguished from

12. William A. Ward, "Economic Evaluation and Efficiency Shadow Pricing: Domestic Price Numeraire," EDI Course Material, CN–2 (Washington, D.C.: World Bank, 1976; processed), p. 36.

intermediate products. Intermediate products are goods that are produced to be used as inputs in a further stage of the project. Thus, if grain produced in a project is sold, it is a final product, and its value would be shown separately as the gross value of production of grain. If, however, it is used to fatten steers, it is an intermediate product. As such, the value of the grain would not be shown as a separate item. Only the gross value of production of steers would be shown; to include the value of grain as well would be double counting. If some of the grain is sold and the rest is fed to steers, only the value of the portion sold should be shown as the gross value of production of grain.

Water presents another interesting example. Drinking water is a final product, but irrigation water is an intermediate product used to increase agricultural production, which is the final product of an irrigation project. Therefore, in the analysis of an irrigation project, the water produced is not valued. Instead, the value of agricultural products consumed and sold is used to calculate the gross value of production.

Intangible benefits

Intangible benefits of a project are those which represent a true value but which are not incorporated in the analysis because they are difficult to value. This category includes such benefits as health, education, nutrition, recreation, and social welfare. Attempts to value these benefits have not been satisfactory, and it is generally felt that the financial or economic analysis is usually not appropriate for dealing with them.

Different approaches may be taken to deal with intangible benefits which represent only a small part of the total benefits and with those which form a major part. If the intangible benefits are insignificant, they may be ignored, and the project may be analyzed in the usual way. When the project appears to be marginal, however, the intangible benefits may then be assessed subjectively to determine whether or not the project should be implemented. Similarly, if two projects are equally profitable, subjective assessment of the intangible benefits accruing from both projects may help to determine which project to implement.

When intangible benefits account for most of the project benefits, as could be the case in rural development projects, the normal method of analysis would place the project at a disadvantage, because costs are included, but most benefits are omitted. In this case the components of the project with quantifiable benefits should be separated from those with intangible benefits. Then the usual techniques of economic analysis should be applied to the former, and least-cost analysis to the latter. In the least-

Figure 8–1. *Transition from Financial to Economic Analysis*

ADJUSTMENTS

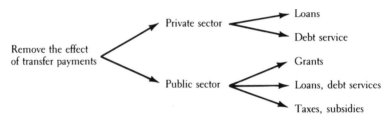

Remove distortions in the prices of:

Foreign exchange

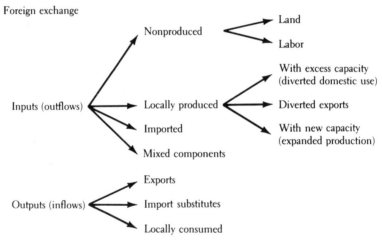

ADDITIONS

Off-farm investment costs
Research, extension, and training costs
Administration costs

cost analysis, benefits are assumed to be at a certain level, and the most efficient method to reach that level has to be found. If there are quantifiable benefits in the components analyzed by the least-cost method, they should be subtracted from the annual costs before discounting.

Aggregating Data for Economic Analysis

The economic analysis incorporates the off-farm investment costs and the provision of common services (such as roads, bridges, and water supply), which are not reflected in the financial analysis, as well as the aggregate value of inputs and outputs for all the farms participating in the project. There is no standard method for aggregating these data. Generally, two approaches are used: aggregating farm models and aggregating enterprise budgets. The steps involved in the transition from financial to economic analysis are shown in Figure 8–1.

Aggregating farm models

Chapter 6 recommended that a project be divided into models, each representing reasonably homogenous groups of farms. The purpose of this is twofold: to assess the effect of the project on each group of farmers and to facilitate the preparation of the economic analysis.

Chapter 7 recommended that a financial analysis for the farm family be prepared for each model. Since the economic analysis represents the aggregation of all the farms in the project, the financial analysis for each model may be used as the basis for aggregation. Simply multiply each item of cost and benefit in the model by the number of farms it represents, then add together the total for each model. If market prices reflect true economic values, off-farm costs may be added and transfer payments, loans, grants, and debt service subtracted to arrive at the economic analysis. Since market prices often fail to reflect true economic values, however, it would be necessary to adjust the values of inputs and outputs before aggregating the data and calculating the economic rate of return. This is a relatively simple exercise when there are few adjustments. But when there are many, complicated adjustments, the financial analysis for each model has to be recast in economic values before the aggregation.

One very important, but often overlooked, aspect of project analysis is the phasing of the project. Because of physical characteristics, the capacity of the project staff, and the rate of acceptance by the farmer, most projects cannot be fully implemented by the end of the first year. The prudent analyst must allow for this factor.

Two aspects of project phasing should be recognized. The first relates to the effect of the project on the farm; the second, to the number of new farms that enter the project each year during its implementation. The effect of the project on the farm is reflected in the rate of change in the composition and size of enterprises and in the level of productivity. This aspect does not require special treatment, since the characteristics of each farm determine the model to which the farm is related. The entry of new farms into the project each year, however, requires special attention.

This point may be illustrated by the two components in the Philippines second livestock development project discussed in Chapter 6: expanding broiler capacity on 250 farms from 4,000 to 8,000 birds, and increasing the laying flock on another 150 farms from 4,000 to 8,000 layers. The broiler component is to phase-in eighty farms each in the first two years and ninety farms in the third. The egg production component is to be implemented at the rate of fifty farms each year during the first three years. In aggregating each model, it must be remembered that all the farms do not begin participating in the project in year 1. Since this analysis assumes that all the farms would continue to produce at a constant level without the project, the second group of farms that would enter the project in year 2 would produce at the same level in year 1 as they would without the project; and the third group would do so in the first two years. In effect, the incremental net benefit would be shown as zero in the analysis until the farms begin to participate in the project.

If it is inappropriate to assume that costs and benefits would remain constant without the project, two accounts should be prepared for each model: one showing the projection of costs and benefits without the project; the other, with the project. Until a particular group of farms enters the project, the costs and benefits with the project should be shown at the same level as those without the project, to allow for the fact that not all farms participate during the first year.

Terminal phasing is sometimes introduced to compensate for the phasing at the beginning of the project. For example, if a project that takes three years to implement has a life of fourteen years, the analysis would extend for sixteen years to incorporate the farms entering the project in the second and third years for the total period.[13] Alternatively there could be one termination date for all the farms. This would mean that some farms would not be reflected in the analysis for the full life of the project. For example, if the life of the project is twenty years, farms that enter the

13. World Bank, "Appraisal for an Agricultural Development Project—The Gambia," PA–142a (a restricted circulation document) (Washington, D.C., 1972; processed); Table 6.

project in the second year would be included in the analysis for only nineteen years, and farms that enter in the third year, for eighteen years, and so forth.

Aggregating enterprise budgets

In some projects, farm size and production patterns vary so widely that it would be impossible to prepare representative farm models. In these cases, the economic analysis is prepared by aggregating the enterprise budgets. Budgets usually show the costs and returns per acre (or other unit of land area) for each enterprise under various levels of management. Market prices are usually used, and they must be adjusted where necessary to reflect the economic valuation of costs and benefits. The data in the enterprise budgets are then multiplied by the area represented by each level of management, and then are aggregated to provide the basis for the economic analysis.

Format for Economic Analysis

There is no standard format for laying out the economic analysis of a project. Table 8–3 shows one approach. Several alternative forms of presentation are commonly used. In some instances, the axes in Table 8–3 are reversed, with the "items" shown on the horizontal axis and the period of the project life shown on the vertical axis. Quite often too, only three items are shown: incremental cost, incremental benefit, and incremental net benefit, as illustrated in the following example:

Year	Incremental cost	Incremental benefit	Incremental net benefit
1	10,000	0	− 10,000
2	1,000	2,000	1,000
3	1,500	3,000	1,500
4	2,000	4,000	2,000
5	2,000	4,000	2,000
6–10	2,000	4,000	2,000

The incremental cost is calculated by subtracting total costs without the project from total costs with the project for each year over the life of the project. Incremental benefit is the difference between total benefits with and without the project. The incremental net benefit is the difference between incremental costs and incremental benefit.

Table 8–3. *Format for Economic Analysis*

Item	Without project	With project (year)		
		1	2	3
(a) Benefits				
Gross value of production				
Rental value of farmhouse				
Salvage values				
Other benefits				
Total				
(b) Costs				
Investment off-farm				
Investment on-farm				
Research, extension, and training				
Administration				
Production				
Other				
Total				
(c) Net benefit (a − b)[a]				
(d) Net benefit without project[b]				
(e) Incremental net benefit[c] (cash flow) (c − d)				
Economic rate of return = __ percent				

a. Includes compensation for (a) capital existing without the project, (b) owned land, (c) family labor and management, and (d) new capital invested in the project.

b. Includes compensation for (a) capital existing without the project, (b) owned land, and (c) family labor and management.

c. Includes (d) compensation for new capital invested in the project only.

For the purpose of exposition, the format shown in Table 8–3 is recommended. This table will be used as the basis for discussing the basic items which are included in the economic analysis.

Benefits

Benefits include the gross value of production, rental value of farmhouses, salvage values, and other miscellaneous benefits. Transfer payments such as grants, subsidies, and loans are excluded.

The gross value of production represents the economic value of output produced in the project. As discussed earlier, project output can be divided into exports, import substitutes, and locally consumed output. Exported output is valued at the export parity price; import substitutes, at the import parity price; and locally consumed output, at the farm gate price.

The rental value of farmhouses represents the imputed value of the benefit the families participating in the project derive from occupying the farmhouses constructed in the project. It is estimated at the rate families would pay normally for comparable housing. If the market for farmhouses is inactive, the rental value may be estimated at from 5 to 10 percent of the cost of construction, depending on the nature of the construction.

Salvage value represents the residual market value of the assets used in the project, as discussed in Chapter 7.

Costs

Costs include investments in infrastructure outside the farm, such as roads, bridges, water supply, and other common services. Expenditure on research, extension, training, and administration, which are not normally included in the financial analysis, are reflected in the economic analysis. So are farm investment costs and production expenses. A less obvious and often neglected item of cost is described as "technical spillover" or "technological externalities."[14] It refers to costs incurred or losses sustained elsewhere in the economy as a consequence of implementing the project. An example is the decrease in honey production resulting from the spraying of crops in an agricultural project. Although the costs—or the benefits foregone—may not be incurred on the project site, they represent real costs to the economy that would not have been sustained without the project. Unlike intangible benefits, these costs can be measured and should be incorporated in the economic analysis.

Project costs are incurred by procuring inputs. As noted earlier, the market prices used in the financial analysis are sometimes inappropriate for the economic analysis. First of all, the effect of all transfer payments, such as customs duties, excise duties, tariffs, land and corporation taxes, sales and other indirect taxes, social security payments, and contribution to pension funds, should be excluded. Also, the valuation of inputs must be adjusted to reflect properly their opportunity cost. They should first be broken down into the four categories mentioned earlier: nonproduced inputs; locally produced inputs; imported inputs; and mixed-component inputs. Each item should then be valued according to the principles discussed before.

Incremental net benefit

The net benefit is obtained by subtracting the costs from the benefits. The incremental net benefit is obtained by subtracting the net benefit

14. Gittinger, *Economic Analysis of Agricultural Projects,* p. 29.

without the project from the net benefit accruing each year with the project. It was stated in Chapter 4 that the net benefit without the project would not necessarily be constant. In fact it is often expected to vary during the life of the project. In this case it would be inappropriate to represent the situation without the project in a single column, as shown in Table 8–3. Instead a separate table has to be prepared, showing the net benefit without the project parallel to that with the project over the life of the project.

Internal economic rate of return

The economic rate of return reflects both the return of capital to recover the resources invested in the project and the return to society's capital invested in the project.

The incremental net benefit stream is usually negative in the early life of the project when costs exceed benefits. It becomes positive in the later years as the project begins to produce benefits that exceed costs. The discount rate that equalizes the present worths of the negative and positive values in the incremental net benefit stream is called the internal economic rate of return. This rate of return may be interpreted as the average rate of interest earned by investing society's capital in the project. If the internal economic rate of return is zero, society would merely recover its investment without earning any interest; if it is greater than zero, society would earn interest in addition to recovering all its investment.

Limitations of the Economic Rate of Return

The economic rate of return has been adopted as the most common measure of project worth by the World Bank and by many other international organizations because it has certain advantages over the benefit/cost ratio and the net present worth. It also has certain limitations, however, that should not be overlooked.

Two principal advantages of the rate of return are that it can be calculated without the opportunity cost of capital, and that it can be used as a basis for ranking projects under certain conditions. The benefit/cost ratio can also be used to rank projects, but different results will be obtained depending on the convention used in netting out costs (Chapter 4). The net present worth is not affected by the convention used in netting out costs, but by the problem of choosing the proper discount rate. It is defective as a measure for ranking projects because it is an absolute, not a relative measure. Thus, for example, a large marginally acceptable project could achieve a higher ranking than several smaller highly attractive ones, which could yield a higher net present worth in aggregate.

Ranking of projects is sometimes useful, but project selection is seldom based merely on ranking by using the rate of return, the benefit/cost ratio, the net present worth, or any other single measure. Indeed, if the objective is merely to decide between accepting or rejecting several projects, the application of the decision criteria for the three measures of project worth (that is, the benefit/cost ratio is greater than one, the net present worth is positive, and the economic rate of return is greater than the opportunity cost of capital) will invariably result in the acceptance of the same projects. If, however, implementation priorities are to be established as well, the economic rate of return is a more reliable indicator, except in three instances: when the incremental net benefit stream has no negative value; when the rate of return is higher than 50 percent; and when comparing mutually exclusive alternatives.

When the incremental net benefit stream has only positive values, the rate of return is undefined and does not provide a basis for making comparisons. Under these circumstances, the net present worth is a more useful basis for comparison. In other cases, the incremental net benefit stream might have some negative values, but the rate of return might be higher than 50 percent. Since most discount tables only carry factors up to 50 percent, it would be impossible to compare two projects with rates of return higher than 50 percent. Here again, the net present worth is a more useful basis for comparison.

Mutually exclusive alternatives[15] arise when only one of several project alternatives can be implemented; selection of any one precludes adoption of any other. Each variation in the design, scale, technology, or timing of a project constitutes a mutually exclusive alternative. Examples include the choice between a small version of a project and a larger, more expensive version of the same project, or between the application of capital-intensive and labor-intensive technology, or between starting the project in one year as against in some other year in the future. In any of these situations, the simple comparison of the economic rates of return for the two alternatives gives misleading results. Two other approaches are recommended. The simple approach is to compare the net present worth of each alternative and to accept the alternative with the highest net present worth. The alternative approach is to discount the difference between the incremental

15. For a fuller discussion, see Gittinger, *Economic Analysis of Agricultural Projects*, chapter 5; also Willard D. Weiss, "Manual on Highway Project Analysis in Developing Countries," prepared for the Economic Development Institute (Washington, D.C.: World Bank, 1974; processed).

net benefit streams of the projects taking two at a time. If the rate of return for the difference between the two streams is greater than the opportunity cost of capital, the larger project with the higher net present worth should be selected in preference to the smaller project with the higher rate of return. If, however, the rate of return for the difference between the two streams is less than the opportunity cost of capital, the smaller project should be selected, because the return from the incremental investment in the larger project would be less than the minimum acceptable rate of return.

A simple hypothetical example comparing a small mutually exclusive project with a larger, more expensive alternative is illustrated in Table 8–4. Assuming an opportunity cost of capital of 12 percent, the net present

Table 8–4. *Comparison of Mutually Exclusive Alternatives*

	Year		
Item	1	2–10	Total
Economic return from the small project			
Net benefit (dollars)	− 50,000	+ 15,000	—
Discount factor (12 percent)	0.893	4.757	—
Present worth (dollars)			
12 percent	− 44,650	+ 71,355	+ 26,705
26 percent	− 39,700	+ 40,065	+ 365
27 percent	− 39,350	+ 38,655	− 695

Net present worth at 12 percent = $26,705; economic rate of return = 26 percent.

Economic return for the larger project			
Net benefit (dollars)	− 200,000	+ 50,000	—
Discount factor (12 percent)	0.893	4.757	—
Present worth (dollars)			
12 percent	− 178,600	+ 237,850	+ 59,250
20 percent	− 166,600	+ 167,950	+ 1,350
21 percent	− 165,200	+ 161,400	− 3,800

Net present worth at 12 percent = $59,250; economic rate of return = 20 percent.

Economic return for the difference between net benefits			
Additional net benefit (dollars)	− 150,000	+ 35,000	—
Discount factor (12 percent)	0.893	4.757	—
Present worth (dollars)			
12 percent	− 133,950	+ 166,495	+ 32,545
18 percent	− 127,050	+ 127,645	+ 595
19 percent	− 126,000	+ 122,465	− 3,535

Net present worth at 12 percent = $32,545; economic rate of return = 18 percent.

— Not applicable.

worth is $26,705 for the small project and $59,250 for the larger project. The economic rate of return is 26 percent for the small project and 20 percent for the larger project. If these two projects were independent, implementation of both would be justified, since in each case the rate of return is higher than the opportunity cost of capital. They happen, however, to be mutually exclusive alternatives; implementing one would automatically rule out implementing the other.

If selection were to be made according to the economic rate of return, the smaller project with a 26 percent rate of return would be selected, but this would be incorrect because the economic rate of return for the additional investment of $150,000 to undertake the larger project is higher than the opportunity cost of capital. Thus, the larger project yielding the higher net present worth should be selected.

Sensitivity Analysis

The computation of the benefit/cost ratio, the net present worth, and the internal rate of return in the financial and economic analysis is based on assessing the most probable outcome of many events. Naturally, any weakness in this assessment can cause considerable error, particularly in agricultural projects in which the farmer has virtually no control over his environment. The data used to analyze agricultural projects are affected by varying degrees of uncertainty in predicting prices as well as production. For example, in crop enterprises it is often easy to be overly optimistic about the speed of implementing a project or the rate at which yields are expected to increase as a result of the farmer's acceptance of and responsiveness to improved technology or new cropping systems. Similarly, errors may arise in analyzing livestock enterprises, particularly in forecasting stocking rates, weaning percentages, feed consumption, or increase in meat or milk production. Also difficult to forecast are delays in construction, postponement of benefits, and cost overruns. Moreover, forecasting prices creates considerable problems. Error in forecasting prices is partly minimized by assuming constant prices, but real relative changes could occur in the relation between the prices of inputs and outputs, and this could affect the outcome of the project.

It is prudent, therefore, to identify the crucial factors that can most seriously affect the project and to test the effect of changes in the values of these factors on the original result. This is accomplished by simply reworking the financial and economic analysis, adjusting project costs and benefits to reflect what would happen under a different set of circumstances, and recalculating the benefit/cost ratio, the net present worth, and the internal rate of return under each alternative set of circumstances. This technique is called sensitivity analysis. Sensitivity analysis can be applied to one factor at a time, such as a decrease in the price of the output or an increase in the cost of some critical input. It can also be applied to a combination of changes in the value of several factors.

Sensitivity analysis is an important feature in project analysis in dealing with uncertainty and in drawing attention to critical areas that could affect the success of the project. Thus, if the price of the output is found to be a critical factor, efforts can be made to strengthen the marketing program or to reduce project costs. If the project is sensitive to variation in yields of enterprises, greater attention can be devoted to the extension program, and efforts can be made to improve productivity.

Sensitivity analysis has two major disadvantages.[16] It is incomplete because it is not designed to cope with all possible circumstances; it is also ambiguous in that it does not specify the likelihood of the occurrence of the alternatives. Despite these disadvantages, sensitivity analysis provides sufficient indication of the riskiness of most development projects. Risk analysis is the extension of sensitivity analysis. Jones has proposed a simplified approach to risk analysis "by hand";[17] more elaborate techniques are outlined by Pouliquen[18] and Reutlinger.[19]

---

16. William I. Jones, "Agricultural Development Project (The Gambia): Risk-Analysis Supplement," EDI course material, CN–5 (Washington, D.C.: 1976; processed).
17. Ibid.
18. Louis Pouliquen, *Risk Analysis in Project Appraisal*, World Bank Staff Occasional Papers, no. 11 (Baltimore: Johns Hopkins University Press, 1970).
19. Shlomo Reutlinger, *Techniques for Project Appraisal under Uncertainty*, World Bank Staff Occasional Papers, no. 10 (Baltimore: Johns Hopkins University Press, 1970).

References

.•-•-•··•-•-•.

The word "processed" indicates works that are reproduced by mimeograph, xerography, or another manner other than conventional typesetting and printing.

Brown, Maxwell L. "Philippine Livestock Exercise." EDI course material, AE–1073 P&S. Washington, D.C.: World Bank, 1977. Processed.

Bruce, Colin. "Social Cost-Benefit Analysis: A Guide for Country and Project Economists to the Derivation and Application of Economic and Social Accounting Prices." World Bank Staff Working Paper, no. 239. Washington, D.C.: World Bank, 1976. Processed.

Economic Development Institute. "Appraisal of the Hounslow Irrigation Scheme." prepared by participants in the Agricultural Projects Course. Washington, D.C.: World Bank, 1973. Processed.

———. "Appraisal of Meylersfield Drainage Project." Prepared by participants in the Rural Development Projects Course. Washington, D.C.: World Bank, 1977. Processed.

Edwards, David. *Economic Study of Small Farming in Jamaica*. Kingston University of the West Indies, Institute of Social and Economic Research, 1961.Processed.

Ettinger, Stephen J. "Nigeria: The Opportunity Cost of Rural Labor." Research paper prepared for the World Bank. Washington, D.C., 1973. Processed.

Gittinger, J. Price. "Agricultural Loan Repayment Computation and Review Exercise." EDI course material, AE–1024 P&S. Washington, D.C.: World Bank, 1973. Processed.

———, ed. *Compounding and Discounting Tables for Project Evaluation*. Baltimore: Johns Hopkins University Press, 1973.

———. *Economic Analysis of Agricultural Projects*. Baltimore: Johns Hopkins University Press, 1972.

———— and Janet K. Stockard. "Kitulo Plateau Ranch Herd Building and Stabilization Exercise." EDI course material, AE–1066 P&S. Washington, D.C.: World Bank, 1974. Processed.

Heady, Earl O. and Harold R. Jensen. *Farm Management Economics.* Englewood Cliffs: Prentice-Hall, 1954.

Jones, William I. "Agricultural Development Project (The Gambia): Risk Analysis Supplement." EDI course material, CN–5. Washington, D.C.: World Bank, 1976. Processed.

Kao, Charles H. C., Kurt R. Anschel, and Carl K. Eicher. Disguised Unemployment in Agriculture: A Survey." In *Agriculture in Economic Development,* Edited by Carl Eicher and Lawrence Witt. New York: McGraw-Hill, 1964.

Krishna, Raj. "Agricultural Price Policy and Economic Development." In *Agricultural Development and Economic Growth.* Edited by M. H. Southworth and B. J. Johnston. New York: Cornell University Press, 1975.

Little I. M. D., and J. A. Mirrlees. *Project Appraisal and Planning for the Developing Countries.* London: Heineminn Educational Books, 1974.

Nelson, Aaron G., Warren F. Lee, and William G. Murray. *Agricultural Finance.* 6th ed. Ames: Iowa State University Press, 1973.

Pouliquen, Louis. *Risk Analysis in Project Appraisal.* World Bank Staff Occasional Papers, no. 11. Baltimore: Johns Hopkins Press, 1970.

Raj, James S. "Ratio Analysis." EDI course material, CN–422. Washington, D.C.: World Bank, 1977. Processed.

Reutlinger, Shlomo. *Techniques for Project Appraisal under Uncertainty.* World Bank Staff Occassional Papers, no. 10. Baltimore: Johns Hopkins Press, 1970.

Schaefer-Kehnert, Walter. "How to Start an Internal Rate of Return Calculation." EDI course material, CN–30. Washington, D.C.: World Bank, 1978. Processed.

Schlesinger, Eugene R. "The Use of Numeraires in Social Cost-Benefit Analysis: An Introductory Overview." EDI course material, CN–841. Washington, D.C.: World Bank, 1978. Processed.

Selly, Clifford, and David Wallace. *Planning for Profit.* Farm Economies Branch, School of Agriculture, University of Cambridge, England 1961. Processed.

Spencer, Dunstan S. C. "Micro-Level Farm Mangement and Production Economics Research Among Traditional African Farmers: Lessons from Sierra Leone." African Rural Employment Paper, no. 3. East Lansing, Michigan: Department of Agricultural Economics, Michigan State University, 1972. Processed.

Squire, Lyn, and Herman G. van der Tak. *Economic Analysis of Projects.* Baltimore: Johns Hopkins University Press, 1975.

Ssentongo, Kyeyune. "An Economic Survey of the High Altitude Areas of Ankole." Uganda Ministry of Agriculture, Forestry and Cooperatives, 1973. Processed.

Stanton, B. F. "Second Atlantico Project (Colombia) Case Study on Preparing Budgets for a Period of Years." EDI course material, AC–111–S. Washington, D.C.: World Bank, 1972. Processed.

Tollens, Eric F. "Problems of Micro-Economic Data Collection on Farms in Northern Zaïre." Working Paper, no. 7. East Lansing, Michigan: Department of Agricultural Economics, Michigan State University, 1975. Processed.

United Kingdom, Ministry of Agriculture, Fisheries and Food. *The Farm as a Business.* London: Her Majesty's Stationery Office, 1958.

United Nations Industrial Development Organization. *Guidelines for Project Evaluation.* New York: United Nations, 1972.

Upper, Jack L., and Janet K. Stockard. "Introduction to a Funds Approach to Project Analysis." EDI course material, CN–18. Washington, D.C.: World Bank, 1977. Processed.

Upton, Martin. *Farm Management in Africa.* London: Oxford University Press, 1973.

Ward, William A. "Adjusting for Over-Valued Local Currency: Shadow Exchange Rates and Conversion Factors." EDI course material, CN–28. Washington, D.C.: World Bank, 1976. Processed.

———. "Calculating Import and Export Parity Prices." EDI course material, CN–3. Washington, D.C.: World Bank, 1976. Processed.

Webster's Third International Dictionary. Edited by Phillip Babcock. 7th ed. Springfield, Mass.: G. and C. Merriam, 1966.

Weiss, Willard D. "Manual on Highway Project Analysis in Developing Countries." Prepared for the Economic Development Institute. Washington, D.C.: World Bank, 1974. Processed.

World Bank. "Appraisal for an Agricultural Development Project—The Gambia." PA–142a. A restricted-circulation document. Washington, D.C., 1972. Processed.

——— "Appraisal of the Second Livestock Development Project—Philippines." 1070–PH. A restricted-circulation document. Washington, D.C., 1976.

———. "Appraisal of Upper Egypt Drainage Project." 80a-UAR. A restricted-circulation document. Washington, D.C., 1973. Processed.

———. "Bank Policy on Agricultural Credit." 436. A restricted-circulation document. Washington, D.C., 1974. Processed.

———. "Second Atlantico Development Project—Colombia." PA–846.

A restricted-circulation document. Washington, D.C., 1972. Processed.

————. "Tamil Nadu Agricultural Credit Project—India."PA–81a. A restricted-circulation document. Washington, D.C., 1971. Processed.

Yang, W. Y. *Methods of Farm Management Investigations*. Rome: Food
and Agricultural Organization, 1965.

The full range of World Bank publications, both free and for sale is described in the *Catalog of World Bank Publications*, and of the continuing research program of the World Bank, in *World Bank Research Program: Abstracts of Current Studies*. The most recent edition of each is available without charge from:

PUBLICATIONS UNIT
THE WORLD BANK
1818 H STREET, N.W.
WASHINGTON, D.C. 20433
U.S.A.